# *The Universal Book of Craft Freemasonry*

(9th Edition 1988)

COPYRIGHT

CONTAINING

THE RITUALS OF THE CEREMONIES

OF

INITIATION, PASSING & RAISING

ALSO

THE CHARGES OF EACH DEGREE

AND

EXPLANATION OF THE TRACING BOARDS

INCLUDING

INSTALLATION OF MASTER

AND

FULL INVESTITURE OF OFFICERS

PRESENTATION OF GRAND LODGE CERTIFICATE

Lewis Masonic

Ninth pocket edition first published 1988
Reprinted 2002, 2004, 2008, 2011, 2014
This Large Print edition first published 2018

ISBN 978 0 85318 559 8



Published by Lewis Masonic
an imprint of Ian Allan Publishing Ltd,
Addlestone, Surrey KT15 2SF

Printed in England

Visit the Lewis Masonic website at www.lewismasonic.co.uk

## *Information for Candidates.*

Freemasonry consists of a body of men banded together to preserve the secrets, customs, and ceremonials handed down to them from time immemorial, and for the purposes of mutual, intellectual, social, and moral improvement; they also endeavour to cultivate and exhibit brotherly love, relief and truth, not only to one another, but to the world at large.

Freemasonry offers no pecuniary advantages whatever, neither does there exist any obligation nor implied understanding binding one Mason to deal with another, nor to support him in any way in the ordinary business relations of life.

Freemasonry teaches us to remember our common origin; it also distinctly enjoins us to respect all social distinctions, so that while some must rule, others must obey and cheerfully accept their inferior positions.

Freemasonry has certain charities, but it is not in any sense whatever a benefit society, nor is it based upon any calculations which would render this possible. The charities are solely for *those who having been in good circumstances* have been overtaken by misfortune or adversity, and they are quite insufficient to meet even these demands now made upon them.

Freemasonry distinctly teaches that a man's first duty is to *himself, his wife, his family, and his connections*, and no one should join the Order who cannot well afford to pay the initiation fees and subscriptions to his Lodge, as well as to the Masonic charities, and this without detriment in any way to his comfort, or to that of those who have any claim upon his support.

Freemasonry recognises no distinctions of religion, but none should attempt to enter who have no religious belief, as faith in a Deity must be expressed before any can be initiated, and prayers to Him form a frequent part of the ritual.

Freemasonry, therefore, demands that everyone before offering himself as a candidate, should be well assured in his own mind:-

1. That he sincerely desires the intellectual and moral improvement of himself and his fellow creatures, and that he is willing to devote part of his time, means, and efforts, to the promotion of brotherly love, relief, and truth.
2. That he seeks no commercial, social, nor pecuniary advantages.
3. That he is able to afford the necessary expenditure without injury to himself or connections.
4. That he is willing to enter into solemn obligations in the sight of his God.

## *Preface.*

The Universal Ritual Association was inaugurated at a Meeting held on January 31st, 1966, at Freemasons' Hall, Great Queen Street, W.C.2. The Committee of the Association in conjunction with the Publishers introduce this 9th edition with every confidence, feeling sure that it will meet with the approval of English-speaking Freemasons who practise "Universal Ritual".

Great care has been taken in the compilation to preserve the ancient landmarks, and the established customs of the Order have been rigidly adhered to.

Although the Rubrics are re-written, the actual wording of the Ritual remains unaltered, with the exception of Removal of Penalties from Obligations (as recommended and approved at the Quarterly Communication of Grand Lodge on 11 June 1986).

The Authors hope it will be found to be a work which will appeal to all those desirous of making themselves proficient in the beautiful “Universal Ritual” that has been handed down to us.

# *Index.*

## *General Instructions.*

1. The Brethren must sign the Attendance Book, in the appropriate section according to rank or office, before entering the Lodge Room. It is of great assistance to the Secretary for the writing to be legible.

2. In Universal Lodges it is recommended that both the Wardens' Columns be horizontal before the Lodge is Open and after it is closed.

The Columns should indicate three states of the Lodge:–

| | |
|---|---|
| a. Both columns horizontal. | Lodge closed. |
| b. J. W.'s horizontal and S. W.'s perpendicular. | Lodge at Labour. |
| c. J. W.'s perpendicular and S. W.'s horizontal. | Lodge still open, but at Refreshment. |

3. The Lodge may be "Called Off" in either of the three degrees, but it is generally simpler to resume in the First Degree before doing so. If "Called Off" in a superior degree it is essential that the W. M. shall satisfy himself that all present are qualified in that Degree before "Calling On".

4. The Brethren being assembled in the Lodge Room, the D. C. enters and says:– Brethren, be upstanding to receive the W. M. and his Wardens. Under the Rule that the W. M. should be the last to enter and subsequently the first to leave the Lodge Room, the recommended order of Procession is as follows:–

J. W. J. D. A. D. C.<br>
W. M. *(with Warrant)* →<br>
S. W. S. D. D. C.

The Procession passes up the N. side of the Lodge and the wands are arched for the W. M. to enter his Pedestal.

It is not necessary for the D. C. to "hand-in" the Master or to hand him the G . . l, as the W. M. occupies his position by right. The Procession continues, and s . . . g the Lodge, similarly escorts the J. and

S. Wdns. In the interest of expediency it is considered permissible for the J. W. to enter his Pedestal before the S. W., as it saves one perambulation.

5. According to "Points of Procedure" in the Masonic Year Book, the W. M. decides whether or no gloves are to be worn. If so decreed they are worn by all except the Candidate. The W. M. and Wdns. should not remove them when entrusting or examining the Candidate. The Master Elect should remove them while taking his Ob . .

6. Whenever the W. M. sounds his G . . l the S. and J. Wdns. must respond, except when the W. M. summons the T . . The knocks should be at regular intervals, except as otherwise demanded by the Rubrics or Ritual.

7. From the time the W. M. calls the Brethren "to order" at the Opening, it is the Rule that a Brother takes the Stp. and shews the appropriate Sn. while being addressed by, or addressing the W. M. or his Wdns.; except as otherwise directed in the Rubrics.

It is sufficient for a Brother who has to

speak at length to salute at the beginning and ending of his address.

8. In Universal working it is claimed, that the Candidate should be able to immediately identify the book on which he has taken his Ob.; he cannot therefore be expected to read it upside down.
The oldest illustrations always shew the arrangements of the T. Gt. Lts. with the S. in the lower position on the pages; it therefore follows that the p . . ts of the S. and Cs. should be towards the W. and the S. Ws. readable by the Candidate.
There is no authority for insisting that the V. of the S. L. should be open at any particular chapter or page.

9. All Masonic Sns. should be given silently, even when given as greetings. In each degree, except when given "in Passing", the Sns. are preceded by the Stp. The token of Reverence, usually called the Sn. of Reverence, is not an exclusively Masonic Sn. and is not to be preceded by the Stp. . As the Can. is not instructed in this Sn. in any ceremony, it ought to be explained to him by his Proposer as soon as possible after his initiation. It is given

by placing the Rt. Hd. on the Lt. Bt. with the Tb. concealed behind the Hd. and no Stp. is taken. It is never cut, but gently lowered. It is used during the Prayers and at the Closing in the First Degree. when the I. P. M. says, F. F. F.; it may also be shewn at the end of the Charge after Initiation, and at another point in the Third Degree. The Candidate should not be induced to use it until after the Ceremony of Initiation.

It is recommended that the Brethren shew the Sn. of F. during each Ob.

10. The I. G. makes his reports to the J. W. and W. M., or receives instructions from them, while standing at the N. W. corner, at the Lt. of the S. W. Both the J. W. and I. G. should stand quite square while doing so, turning the head only towards the W. M. or Officer concerned. The I. G. should be the only officer to open and close the door of the Lodge; and he should not cross the threshold when conversing with the T. . The T. enters the Lodge only when summoned by the W. M.; in which case the D. C. receives him and closes the door. The I. G.

temporarily takes the T.'s place outside until he returns. The T. gives one Kk. to indicate that a Brother or Brethren wish to enter the Lodge after it is opened. The I. G. then stands and with Stp. and Sn. reports:– Bro. J. W., there is a report. The J. W. remains seated and after a re-assuring nod from the W. M. gives one Kk. . The I. G. then cuts his Sn. and opens the door, where he receives from the T. the names and rank of the Brother or Brethren seeking admission. He locks the door and returns to report with Stp. and Sn. :– W. M., (*W*) Bro. (*name and rank if higher than P.M.*) seeks admission. (*Grand Officers are announced singly.*)

Members of the Lodge may be announced (*W*) Bro. (*name*) and other Brethren seek admission; but visitors should all be named, as this forms a measure of introduction to the Lodge members.

When the W. M. says:– Admit them Bro. I. G., the I. G. cuts his Sn. and admits them.

The Brethren admitted proceed to the Lt. of the S. W. and salute the W. M. with Stp. and Sn. . Should the Lodge be open in a superior degree, they must first take Stp. and Sn. of the former degree or degrees.

The W. M. may then say "I greet you well Brethren, or Bro. (*name*)".

The D. C. and A. D. C. should be in readiness to conduct Officers of Rank and Visiting Brethren to their appropriate seat in the Lodge.

Brethren wishing to leave the Lodge before it is closed must first ask permission of the W. M. . They then proceed to the Lt. of the S. W. and salute with the Stp. and Sn. only of the degree in which the Lodge is open. (*Pl. Sn. only in Third Degree.*)

A Brother re-entering the Lodge, other than the Can. in the second Degree, need only salute with the Stp. and Sn. of the degree in which it is open (*Pl. Sn. only in Third Degree*) and should be announced:– Bro. (*name*) on his return.

The prefix "Worshipful" is only to precede a Brother's actual name; it should never be used when addressing an Officer as such. To say W. Bro. I. P. M. is incorrect; it should be Bro. I. P. M., but it is correct to say W. Bro. Jones, or W. Bro. Henry Jones.

11. The Brethren who bear Wands should carry them at all times when leaving their appointed positions in Lodge, except when performing the duties of the Ballot Box and when attending to certain duties in the Third Degree. An Officer carrying a Wand does not salute when crossing the E. except in the actual Ceremonies when conducting a Candidate. The Wand should be carried upright and with dignity, it ought never to be leaned on or laid on the ground. The Lodge should be S . . . d at all times, except that the D. C. and A. D. C. are excused from too rigid adherence to this rule.

12. The Deacons speak aloud the words that are called for in the Ritual, except that when the answer the Candidate is expected to give is short, for example:– I do, I will, I am, or I would, he is given a reasonable opportunity to reply before a prompt is given.

At all times the Deacon in charge may whisper such instructions as he may deem conducive to smooth working.

The Deacon should take the Stp. and shew the Sn. together with the Candidate as an example, during the entrusting by the W. M. and the subsequent examinations by the Wdns., also when the Can. retires and enters the Lodge. During the Prayers and Obs. the Deacons should carefully balance their Wands to form a symmetrical triangle over the Can.'s Hd. with the Wand of the Deacon in charge in front.

The general rule that all movements in Lodge should be in the clockwise direction is inevitably broken while taking the Stps. in the Second Degree; because of this it is permissible for the Deacons to turn the Candidate with a forward Lt. wheel, when handing him to the S. W. for presentation to the W. M. .

According to the Rubrics in previous editions of the Universal Ritual Book, the duty of changing the Tracing Boards is allocated to the S. D.; which seems to indicate that the appropriate place for the Boards is leaning against the J. W.'s Pedestal. This procedure has been maintained in the new 9th Edition. It has the advantage, that the T. B. is usually visible to Brethren entering the Lodge; but the disadvantage, that it is out of sight of

the Brethren occupying the S. side.
Remembering the introduction of Tracing Boards, as we know them, came into being after the practice of chalking the emblems on the floor was discontinued, it is probably more historically correct, that the T. B. should be laid in the centre of the floor, the two T. B.s not in use being left at the J. W.'s Pedestal. This is just a little more difficult for the S. D. to do gracefully, but feasible.
A more acceptable way, is to have provided a low stand to support the Boards horizontally in the centre, with a shelf underneath to carry the 1st/2nd boards at such times as the 2nd/3rd are exhibited.
To change the T. B.s under these conditions it is considered desirable for the J. D. to assist the S. D.; so that the principle of not discarding the Wand can be adhered to.
The Opening and Closing can be further implemented by the two Deacons advancing to the E. after arranging the T. B. and crossing Wands above the I. P. M., while he adjusts the three Gt. Ls. .
Although the above is not essential

Universal Practice, it cannot be objected to, should a particular Lodge decide to adopt it.

13. The Ballot is to be taken under the supervision of the D. C., who may delegate the duties as follows:–

The J. D., commencing with the W. M., distributes the tokens.

The D. C. takes the Box to the W. M., who after inspection holds up the nay drawer and shews or declares it to be clear.

While the above proceeds, the Secretary reads the Proposal Form.

The S. D., commencing with the W. M., passes round with the Ballot Box; taking care to hold it quite level. The W. M. finally sounds his G . . . l, repeated by the S. and J. Wdns. and declares the result of the Ballot.

It is preferable that the result of a ballot, vote or election should not be announced as unanimous; because in a large gathering it is not certain that every Brother has exercised the right to cast his vote. It is better to say:– Brethren, I declare the Ballot to be in favour of Mr. (*name*).

14. The pronunciation of the word

"Hele" has long been debated. It is a good old English word derived from the Saxon "Helan" and means to cover. In Universal Working we pronounce it "Heel" not "Hail". No doubt in olden times it was pronounced "Hail", but then the words "conceal" and "reveal" were similarly broadened. There can be little doubt that the compilers of the early ritual intended the three words to form a rhyming assonance.

15. It is better that the W. M. should not say:– "I vacate the Chair in favour of W. Bro. X.", when a P. M. is to conduct a ceremony; but rather, "Brethren, I invite W. Bro. X. to occupy the Chair for the purpose of, etc."

If it is for a superior degree, the W. M. is advised to ask the questions and himself open the Lodge in the requisite degree, before handing over. The W. M. continues to wear his Collar and Gauntlets and sits in the Chair normally occupied by the I. P. M. *(see Masonic Year Book: points of procedure)*. It is quite in order for the temporary occupant to say:– "I now have pleasure in vacating the Chair in favour of the W. M."; together with his few words of thanks, when it is time for the W. M. to return.

16. All questions, remarks, propositions, etc., must be addressed to the W. M. and not to individual officers or members.

17. At the risings, the W. M. should say:– "Brethren, I rise for the (1st., 2nd., or 3rd.) time to enquire if any Brother has aught to propose for the good of Freemasonry in general, or this the *(full name of Lodge)* number *(e. g.)* Four Thousand, two hundred and seventy-five in particular." *(Never quote the figures only, as 4275.)*

18. The recommended order of Recession is as follows:–

| | | | | | | |
|---|---|---|---|---|---|---|
| | P. G. O. | | J. W. | | J. D. | A. D. C. |
| Distinguished Visitors | | Gd. Officers | | W. M. | | → |
| | L. G. R. | | S. W. | | S. D. | D. C. |

*(Brethren are advised to familiarise themselves with the "Points of Procedure", Masonic Year Book; particular attention is drawn to the use of "Vocal Music in Lodge Ceremonies".)*

## *Ceremony of Opening the Lodge in the First Degree.*

*(The Brethren being assembled, the Procession enters the Lodge Room, and the W. M., the J. W. and S. W. are escorted to their Pedestals. The Escort disperses during the second perambulation.)*

W. M.– Brethren, in accordance with Rule 101, Book of Constitutions, I display the Warrant of the Lodge. *(The I. P. M. may assist the W. M. to do this.)*

W. M.– Brethren, we will sing the Opening Ode. *(Where facilities exist.)*

*(The W. M. sounds his G . . l, which is repeated by the S. and J. Wdns. .)*

W. M.– Brethren, assist me to Open the Lodge.

W. M. to J. W.– Bro. *(name)* what is the first care of every Freemason?

J. W.– *(No Stp. or Sn.)* To see that the Lodge is properly T . . d.

W. M.– Direct that duty to be done.

J. W. to I. G.– Bro. *(name)* see that the Lodge is properly T . . d.

*(The I. G. goes to the Door and gives one K. and being answered by the T., confirms that the door is locked and returns to the Lt. of the S. W. .)*

I. G. to J. W.– *(No Stp. or Sn. .)* Bro. *(name)* the Lodge is properly T . . d.

J. W. to W. M.– *(G . . ls once, no Stp. or Sn. .)* Bro. *(name)* the Lodge is properly T . . d.

W. M. to S. W.– Bro. *(name)* the next care?

S. W.– To see that none but Freemasons are present.

W. M.– To order, Brethren, as Freemasons. *(All stand to order with Stp. and Sn. .)*

W. M.– Bro. J. W., how many principal officers are there in the Lodge?

J. W.– Three: the W. M., the S. and J. Wardens.

W. M.– Bro. S. W., how many assistant officers are there?

S. W.– Three, besides the T. or O. G., namely, the S. and J. Deacons and the I. G.

W. M. to J. W.– The situation of the T.?

J. W.– Outside the door of the Lodge.

W. M.– His duty?

J. W.– Being armed with a d . . n s . . d, to keep off all cowans and intruders to Freemasonry, and see that the Candidates are properly prepared.

W. M. to S. W.– The situation of the I. G.

S. W.– Within the entrance of the Lodge.

W. M.– His duty?

S. W.– To admit Freemasons on proof, receive candidates in due form, and obey the commands of the J. W. .

W. M. to J. W.– The situation of the J. D.?

J. W.– At the right of the S. W. .

W. M.– His duty?

J. W.– To carry all messages and communications of the W. M. from the S. to the J. W., and see that the same are punctually obeyed.

W. M. to S. W.– The situation of the S. D.?

S. W.– At, or near, the right of the W. M. .

W. M.– His duty?

S. W.– To bear all messages and commands from the W. M. to the S. W., and await the return of the J. D. .

W. M.– Bro. J. W., your situation in the Lodge?

J. W.– In the S., W. M. .

W. M.– Why are you placed there?

J. W.– To mark the Sun at the meridian, to call the Brethren from labour to refreshment, and from refreshment to labour, that profit and pleasure may be the result.

W. M.– Bro. S. W., your situation in the Lodge?

S. W.– In the W., W. M. .

W. M.– Why are you placed there?

S. W.– To mark the setting Sun, and to close the Lodge by command of the W. M., having seen that every Brother has had his due.

W. M. to I. P. M.– Bro. I. P. M., the Master's place in the Lodge?

I. P. M.– In the E., W. M. .

W. M.– Why is he placed there?

I. P. M.– As the Sun rises in the E. to open and enliven the day, so is the W. M.

placed in the E. to open the Lodge, and employ and instruct the Brethren in Freemasonry.

W. M.– Brethren, the Lodge being duly formed, before I declare it open *(Chaplain, if one appointed; or W. M.)* let us invoke the assistance of T. G. A. O. T. U. on all our undertakings; may our labours, thus begun in order, be conducted in peace, and closed in harmony. *(So mote it be, may be sung.)*

W. M.– Brethren, in the name of T. G. A. O. T. U., I declare the Lodge duly open, for the purpose of Freemasonry in the First Degree.

*(All cut the Sn. The W. M. sounds the Ks. of the D., which are repeated by the S. and J. Wdns., the I. G. and T., at regular intevals. The S. W. raises his Cn. . The S. D. crosses the E. and attends to the T. B. . The I. P. M. steps out as the S. D. passes and opens the V. of the S. L.; it is immaterial at which Chapter it is open, as the entire volume is the first G. Lt. in Freemasonry. The I. P. M. arranges the S. and Cs.; b. p. c. . The S. V. should be placed to be readable by the Can., with the*

*point of the S. towards the W. . The I. P. M. takes one pace backwards, salutes in the first D. and returns. The S. D. should arrange the T. B. immediately the J. W. has given his Ks. . The Brethren all sit, after the W. M. has taken his seat, not before.)*

End of the Ceremony of
Opening in the First Degree.

*(The W. M. sounds his G . . l, which is repeated by the S. and J. Wdns. only.)*

W. M.– Brethren. I now call upon our Bro. Secretary, to read the Minutes of the last Regular Lodge Meeting.

*(This being done, the W. M. says:–)*

Brethren, will all who deem those Minutes worthy of confirmation, please signify in the manner usually observed among Freemasons.

*(Only the Brethren who were present at the last meeting should vote.)*

W. M.– Any to the contrary?

*(Assuming the minutes are confirmed.)*

W. M.– Brethren, I declare the Minutes confirmed.

*(The S. D., without command, and squaring the Lodge, takes the Minute Book to the W. M. for his signature; subsequently retuming it to the Secretary.)*

## *Special Notes on the First Degree.*

It is the responstbility of the W. M. to ensure that the Rules of the Book of Constitutions and the By-laws of the Lodge, in respect of Initiation are strictly observed.

1. The Candidate must always sign the usual Declaration *(rule 162, B. of Cons.)* before the Ceremony can take place.
It is advised that the Candidate be balloted for at the meeting prior to that at which his Initiation is to take place, whenever this is possible.

2. The Proposer and Seconder should make it their business to ensure that the Candidate receives instruction according to "Information for Candidates" on Page iii. After the Ceremony, they should also endeavour to impart instruction so that the

new Brother can intelligently learn the answers to the questions that will be put to him before he is passed to the Second Degree.

3. The preparation of the Candidate by the T . . r is of great importance. It is advisable that the Candidate's pockets be emptied and the contents securely deposited. Should it be impossible to remove a ring, it can be covered with adhesive tape or a bandage. The c . . . t . . . should hang down the back. The colloquy between the T . . r and I. G. should be audible from within the Lodge, during which the latter assures himself that the Candidate is correctly prepared. Neither the T . . r or I. G. should cross the threshold of the Lodge.

4. Before the admission of the Candidate, the I. P. M. should place the W. Ts ready together with an extra p . . r of Cs. and also make sure that the Warrant, Book of Constitutions and Lodge By-laws are to hand.

5. The duties of the J. D. in this Ceremony are amongst the most important in all Freemasonry. He must remember,

especially in the early part, that the Candidate needs his undivided care and attention. He must prompt audibly the instructions called for in the Ritual and in a whisper such further instructions and words of encouragement he may deem necessary. He assists the Candidate to k . . . for the Prayer, but should not induce him to shew the Sn. of R.

An approved method of holding the Candidate is as follows:– The J. D. holds the Can.'s Rt. Hd. firmly in his Lt.; the Lt. arm of the J. D. being between the Rt. arm and body of the Can. . By this method complete control is obtained. Until the R . . . . . of the . . . . . . . , the J. D. never leaves hold of the Can.'s Rt. Hd. except to place it in the clasp of another officer, or while the Can. k . . s for the Prayer and Ob. . The J. D. must be alert to receive back the Can's Rt. Hd. at the appropriate time.

It is advisable for the J. D. to carefully rehearse the Stps, so that neatly done the Can. arrives at the k . . g s . . l in the exact position without further movement.

The r. . .. of the . . . . . requires careful co-

ordination between the W. M. and the J. D. and the I. G. should exactly time his arrival with the p . . . . . . . so that no pause in the proceedings occurs.
It is also advised that the J. D. should undo the c . . t . . rather than take the complete loop over the Can.'s Hd.

6. When the Can. is being entrusted with the W. by the W. M., and subsequently examined by the Wardens, whether it be h . . . d or l . . . d, the complete W. ought not to be repeated in full.
This particular portion of the Ceremony is a lesson to the Candidate as to how he will subsequently use the W., and to repeat it in full is to lose the value of the lesson.

7. It is suggested that storing the B. or A. under the S. W.'s Pedestal lacks dignity; and it is advised that the more ceremonious delivery of it from the E. is useful in emphasising its importance.
There is sometimes a difference of opinion as to whether the E. A. Apron should be worn with the flap up or down. In early Lodges it was often the custom to have a hole in the flap to button it to the wearer's waistcoat.

One theory explains that the flap turned up represents a triangle on a square. which is an ancient symbol indicating that the wearer has not as yet been influenced by the spiritual over the earthly or material subjects, but when at a later date the flap is turned down it signifies the descent of spiritual influence into the material subject, thus marking the Candidate's progress in the Science.

It was said that the raised triangle was an emblem of fire, indicating light, while the lowered triangle was an emblem of water, signifying the flow of intellect.

If this symbolism is recognised in a particular Lodge it should be adhered to and the S. W. should so tie the strings, that the flap remains up throughout the remainder of the Ceremony.

8. When the Candidate, supported by the Deacons, line up at the N. E. corner, it is suggested that it is preferable for the J. D. to hold out his open palm, rather than cause confusion by having a box or plate passed to him. It is for obvious reasons incongruous to use a coin box for this purpose.

9. At the end of the Ceremony, before the Candidate retires, it is a good practice for the W. M. to hand him the question and answer card; and while he is out the T. should instruct him in the Stp. and Sn. .

The Charge after Initiation, while not actually part of the Ceremony, must always be given on the Candidate's return to the Lodge. It is also recommended that the explanation of the First Tracing Board should occasionally be delivered, as it is so instructive to the newly made Freemason.

Finally the Candidate is taken to a seat at the Rt. of the S. D. .

## *Ceremony of Initiation.*

*(The Lodge being open in the First Degree; the Candidate who has been regularly accepted by ballot, must sign the usual Declaration "Rule 162, Book of Constitutions", and be prepared by the T . . When he is ready, the T. gives the report with the 1st D. Ks. .)*

I. G.– *(Advances with Stp. and Sn. .)*

Bro. J. W., there is a report. *(Holds Sn. .)*

J. W.– *(Rises; no Kks. but with Stp. and Sn. .)*

W. M., there is a report. *(Holds Sn.)*

W. M.– Bro. J. W., enquire who wants admission.

J. W.– (Cuts Sn. and Sits.) Bro. I. G., see who seeks admission. *(The I. G. cuts Sn. and goes to the door, which he unlocks.)*

I. G. to T.– Whom have you there? *(The I. G. should keep within the threshold; the*

*T. and Can. remaining just outside; the colloquy should be audible to the Brethren in the Lodge.)*

T. to I. G.– Mr. *(full name)* a poor Candidate in a state of . . . . . . . ., who has been well and worthily recommended, regularly proposed and approved in open Lodge, now comes of his own free will and accord, properly prepared, humbly soliciting to be admitted to the mysteries and privileges of Ancient Freemasonry.

I. G.– How does he hope to obtain those privileges?

T.– By the help of God, being free and of good report.

I. G.– Wait, while I report to the W. M. *(Locks the door, after examining the Can. to see that he is properly prepared.)*

I. G.– *(With Stp. and Sn., at the Lt. of the S. W. .)* W. M., Mr. *(full name)* a poor Candidate in a state of . . . . . . . ., who has been well and worthily recommended, regularly proposed and approved in open Lodge, now comes of his own free will and accord, properly prepared, humbly soliciting to be admitted to the mysteries and privileges of Ancient Freemasonry.

*(Holds Sn. .)*

W. M.– How does he hope to obtain those privileges?

I. G.– By the help of God, being free and of good report. *(Holds Sn. .)*

W. M.– The tongue of good report has already been heard in his favour; do you Brother I. G. vouch that he is properly prepared?

I. G.– I do, W. M. .

W. M.– Admit him in due form.

*(The I. G. cuts his Sn., and the W. M. sounds his G . . l, which is repeated by the S. and J. Wdns. .)*

W. M.– Brother Deacons. *(The I. G. opens the door, and the Deacons receive the Candidate from the T. . The J. D. takes the Can.'s Rt. Hd. in his Lt.; the I. G. applies the . . . . . . . to the Can.'s n. l. b. and asks:–)*

I. G. to Can.– Do you feel anything?

*(On receiving a reply in the affirmative, the I. G. raises the . . . . . . . above his head to shew the W. M. that the Can. has been admitted in "due form". The J. D. leads the Can. to the Lt. of the S. W. . The A. D. C. places the k . . g s . . l in position*

*and the I. G. locks the door.)*

W. M. to Can.– Mr. *(surname)* as no person can be made a Freemason unless he is free, and of mature age, I demand, are you a free man, and of the full age of twenty-one years?

Can. *(Prompted only if really necessary.)* I am.

W. M.– Thus assured, you will kneel, while the blessing of Heaven is invoked in aid of our proceedings.*

*(The Can. is assisted to kneel, on both Ks. .) (The W. M. sounds his G . . l, which is repeated by the S. and J. Wdns. . All rise, with the exception of the Can. and shew the Sn. of R. . During the Prayer, the Deacons stand slightly behind the Can., with their Wands crossed; the J. D.'s in front of the S. D.'s. The Can. should not be induced to shew the Sn. of R. . )*

*(W. M. or Chaplain, if one appointed.)*

**Should the Candidate be a Jew, the W. M. says:– "As an Israelite you will be covered".*

PRAYER

Vouchsafe Thine aid, Almighty Father,

Supreme Governor of the Universe to our present convention, and grant that this Candidate for Freemasonry may so dedicate and devote his life to Thy service, as to become a true and faithful Brother among us. Endue him with a competency of Thy Divine Wisdom, so that, assisted by the secrets of our Masonic art, he may be the better enabled to unfold the beauties of true Godliness, to the honour and glory of Thy Holy Name.

*(So mote it be, which may be sung.)*

W. M. to Can.– Mr. *(surname)* in all cases of difficulty and danger, in whom do you put your trust?

Can.– *(Whispered prompt by J. D.)* In God.

W. M.– Right glad am I to find your faith so well founded; relying on such sure support, you may rise and *(If the Can. is a Jew, omit the words "rise and")* follow your leader with a firm but humble confidence, for where the name of God is invoked, we trust no danger will ensue. *(The Ds. lower Wands.)*

*(It is usual to drop, but not cut, the Sn. of R. after the word "God". The Brethren*

*sit, after the W. M., and the A. D. C. removes the k . . g s . . l.)*

W. M.– *(Sounds his G . . l, repeated by the S. and J. Wdns. .)* Brethren in the N. E. S. and W., take notice, that Mr. *(name in full)* is about to pass in view before you, to show that he is a Candidate properly prepared to be made a Freemason.

*(The J. D. takes the Can. by the Rt. Hd., and says audibly:–)*

J. D. to Can.– S. O. W. T. L. F. *(They proceed along the N. side, the S. D. follows and resumes his seat. The Can. is taken to the J. W., and with the Can.'s Rt. Hd., the J. D. gently S . . the J. W.'s Rt. Sr. T. T. . )*

J. W. to J. D.– Whom have you there?

J. D. to J. W.– *(With Stp. and Sn., but retaining hold of the Can.'s Rt. Hd. .)* Mr. *(name in full)* a poor Candidate, etc. *(Continue with same report as I . G. .)*

J. W.– How does he hope to obtain those privileges?

J. D.– By the help of God, being free and of good report. *(Cuts Sn. .)*

J. W.– *(Rises, and takes the Can.'s Rt. Hd. from the J. D. .)* Enter, free and of good report.

*(The J. D. receives back the Can.'s Rt. Hd. and conducts him to the S. W., where a similar examination is gone through; after this the S. W. remains standing, and the Can. is taken past the Pedestal, and with a forward left wheel the J. D. places the Can.'s Rt. Hd. in the S. W.'s Lt. . The J. D. arranges the Can. to face E., and stands at his Lt. .)*

S. W.– *(With Stp. and Sn.)* W. M., I present to you Mr. *(name in full)* a Candidate properly prepared to be made a Freemason. *(Holds Sn. .)*

W. M.– Bro. S. W., your presentation shall be attended to, for which purpose I will address a few questions to the Candidate, which I trust he will answer with candour.

*(The S. W. cuts his Sn. and the J. D. receives back the Can.'s Rt. Hd.; the J. D. stands at the Can.'s Rt. side and they both face E. . The S. W. sits.)*

W. M. to Can.– Mr. *(surname)* do you seriously declare on your honour that unbiased by the improper solicitation of friends against your own inclination, and uninfluenced by mercenary or other unworthy motives, you freely and voluntarily offer yourself a Candidate for the Mysteries and privileges of Ancient Freemasonry?

Can.– *(Prompted only if really necessary.)* I do.

W. M.– Do you likewise pledge yourself, that you are prompted to solicit those privileges, by a favourable opinion preconceived of the Institution, a general desire for knowledge, and a sincere wish to render yourself more extensively serviceable to your fellow creatures?

Can.– *(Prompted only if really necessary.)* I do.

W. M.– Do you further seriously declare on your honour, that, avoiding fear on the one hand, and rashness on the other, you will steadily persevere through the ceremony of your initiation, and, if admitted, will ever afterwards act and abide by the ancient usages and established customs of the order?

Can.– *(Prompted only if really necessary.)* I do.

W. M. to S. W.– Bro. S. W. *(The S. W. stands, takes Stp. and shews Sn.)* direct the

J. D. to instruct the Candidate to advance to the E. in due form. *(The S. W. cuts his Sn. and sits.)*

S. W. to J. D.– Bro. J.D. *(The J. D. takes Stp. unobtrusively, shews Sn. and turns his Head only towards the S. W., still holding the Can.'s Hd.)* it is the W. M.'s command, that you instruct the Candidate to advance to the E. in due form.

*(The J. D. cuts Sn., and whispering s. o. w. t. l. f., and squaring the turns, conducts the Can. along the N. side of the Lodge and into the centre, about four feet from the k . . g s . . l, facing S. . The J. D. then stands in front of the Can., takes him by both wrists or forearms and directs:–)*

J. D. to Can.– Place your feet together, turn out your Lt. Ft., heel to heel, so as to form a S.; take a short Stp. with your Lt. Ft., dragging the Rt. Ft. after it, heel to heel.

Take another Stp. a little longer, dragging the Rt. Ft. after it, heel to heel.

Take another Stp. longer still, heels together as before.

*(The J. D. should have carefully rehearsed these Stps., so that correctly*

*executed, the Can. is turned to face the W. M. in the exact position for k . . g without further movement. At this point the S. D. takes his position at the Lt. of the Candidate.)*

W. M. to Can.– Mr. (surname) it is my duty to inform you that Masonry is free, and requires a perfect freedom of inclination in every Candidate for its mysteries; it is founded on the purest principles of piety and virtue; it possesses many great and invaluable privileges; and in order to secure those privileges to worthy men, and we trust to worthy men alone, vows of fidelity are required; but let me assure you that in those vows there is nothing incompatible with your civil, moral, or religious duties. Are you therefore willing to take a G. and S. O., founded on the principles I have stated, to keep inviolate the secrets and mysteries of the Order?

Can.– *(Prompted only if necessary.)* I am.

W. M.– Then you will kneel on your Lt. Ke., place your Rt. Ft. so as to form a S., (*Rises*) give me your Rt. Hd., which I place on this book, the V. of the S. L., while your Lt. Hd. will be employed in supporting a pair of . . . . . . . . , one . . . . . . presented to your n. l. b.

*(At the proper time, the J.D. assists the W. M. by lifting the Can.'s Rt. Hd. . The S. D. also lifts the Can.'s Lt. Hd., which the W. M. places on the Can.'s Lt. Bt.; the . . . . . . . open at Rt. Angles are placed in the Can.'s Lt. Hd., one limb hanging down. The W. M. sounds his G . . l, which is repeated by the S. and J. Wdns. . The Brethren all rise and stand to order with the Sn. of F. . The Deacons standing slightly behind the Can., cross their Wands with the J. D.'s in front.)*

W. M. to Can.– State your name at length, and repeat after me:–

### Obligation

W. M.– I *(full name)* in the presence of T. G. A. O. T. U., and of this worthy, worshipful and warranted Lodge of Ancient, Free and Accepted Masons, regularly assembled and properly dedicated, of my own free will and accord, do hereby *(The W. M. touches the Can.'s*

*Rt. Hd. with his Rt. Hd. .)* and hereon, *(The W. M. touches the Can.'s Rt. Hd. and the V. of the S. L. with his Rt. Hd. .)* solemnly and sincerely swear, that I will always hele *(heel)*, conceal, and never reveal, any part or parts, point or points, of the secrets and mysteries of, or belonging to, Free and Accepted Masons in Masonry, which may heretofore have been known by, shall now, or may at any future time be communicated to me, unless it be to a true and lawful Brother, or Brethren, and not even unto him or them until after due trial, strict examination, or sure information from some well known Brother, that he or they are worthy of that confidence, or in the body of a just, perfect, and regular Lodge of Ancient Free and Accepted Masons. I likewise solemnly promise that I will not write those secrets, indite, carve, mark, engrave, or otherwise them delineate, or cause or suffer it to be done by others, if in my power to prevent it, on anything movable or immovable under the canopy of Heaven, whereby or whereon, any letter, character, or figure, or the least trace of any letter, character or figure, may become legible or intelligible to myself or to anyone in the world, least our secret art and hidden mysteries, may improperly become known through my unworthiness. These several points I solemnly swear to observe, without evasion, equivocation, or mental reservation of any kind, in the certain knowledge that on the violation of any of them I shall be branded as a willfully perjured individual, devoid of moral worth, and totally unfit to be received into this worshipful Lodge, or any other warranted Lodge, or society of men who prize honour and virtue, above the external advantages of rank and fortune. So help me G . . . , and keep me steadfast in this, the G. and S.O. of an E. A. Freemason.

*(The W. M. removes the Cs. and the S. D. returns the Can.'s Lt. Hd. to his side; the J. D. sees that the Can.'s Rt. Hd. remains on the V. of the S. L. .)*

W. M.– As what you have repeated may be considered only a serious promise, as a pledge of fidelity, and to render it a G. and S.O., you will seal it with your lips on this book, the V. of the S.L. *(Touches C's*

*Hd. and S. L. The Can. does this, assisted by the J. D., only if necessary; the Ds. lower their wands and the Brethren dis. the Sn. .)*

W. M.– Having been kept for a considerable time in a state of d . . . . . . , what in your present condition, is the predominant wish of your heart?

Can.– *(Prompted by J.D.)* . . . . .

W. M.– Bro. J.D., let that blessing be restored to the Candidate.

*(The W. M. takes his G . . l, and at the proper moment the Brethren simultaneously c . . . their Hds. as the J.D. restores the . . . . . . Only if necessary, the J.D. very gently presses the Can.'s Hd. forward, to direct his gaze on the T. G. Ls. .)*

W. M.– Having been restored to the blessings of material . . . . . , I will now direct your attention, to what we consider the three great, though emblematical . . . . . . in Freemasonry; they are the V. of the S. L., the S., and the Cs.; the S. Ws. are to govern our faith, the S. to regulate our actions, and the Cs. to keep us in due bounds with all mankind,

particularly our Brethren in Freemasonry. *(The W. M. should point out each G. Lt., but not remove them. He takes the Can. by the Rt. Hd. and says:–)*
Rise, duly obligated, Brother among Masons.

*(The W. M. and Brethren resume their seats, including the S. D.. The J. D. takes the Can. by the Rt. Hd. and with a Rt. Wheel conducts him to the N. side of the W. M., about three feet from the Pedestal facing S. where he relinquishes the Can.'s Hd., but remains at his side.)*

W. M.– You are now enabled to discover the three . . . . . . . . . . . . . in Freemasonry, which are situated E., S., and W., and are meant to represent the Sun, the Moon, and the Master of the Lodge, the Sun to rule the day, the Moon to govern by night, and the M. to rule and direct his Lodge.

*(W. M. indicates.)*

W. M.– Bro. *(Surname) (This is the first time that the Can. is directly addressed as 'Brother')*; by your meek and candid behaviour this evening, you have, symbolically, escaped two great dangers, but there was a third which, traditionally, would have awaited you until the latest period of your existence. The dangers you have already escaped are those of s. and s. *(The I. G. carefully times his arrival with the P . . . . . . . . . at this point)* for on your entrance into the Lodge this P . . . . . . . . . was presented to your n.l.b. to imply that, had you rashly attempted to rush forward, you would have been an accessory to your own death by s., as the Brother who held it would have remained firm and done his duty *(the J.D. removes the c . . . t . . . by undoing it, and not by taking it over the Can.'s. Hd. , he hands it to the W. M. who reloops it and demonstrates)*. There was likewise this c.t. with a running n. about your neck which would have rendered any attempt at retreat equally fatal. But the danger which, traditionally, would have awaited you until your latest hour, was the physical penalty at one time associated with the Obligation of an E. A. Freemason had you improperly disclosed the secrets of Freemasonry, that of having t.t.c.a. , t.t.t.o.b.t.r. and b.i.t.s.o.t.s. at l.w.m., a.l.a.c.l. f.t.s. , where t.t.r.e.a.f.t.i.t.t.f.h. The inclusion of such a penalty is unnecessary for the Obligation you have taken this evening is binding upon you for so long as you shall live.

Now that you have taken the G. and S.O. of an E. A. Freemason, I am permitted to inform you that there are several Degrees in Freemasonry, with peculiar secrets restricted to each; these, however, are not communicated indiscriminately, but are conferred upon candidates according to merit and ability. I shall, therefore, proceed to entrust you with the secrets of this Degree, or those marks by which we are known to each other, and distinguished from the rest of the world, but must premise for your general information that all Ss., Ls., and Ps., are true and proper signs by which to know a Freemason; you will therefore stand perfectly erect, your feet in the form of a S. *(Can. does so, instructed by the J.D.'s example and whisper if necessary)* your body thus being considered an emblem of your mind, and your feet of the rectitude of your actions. You will now take a s. s. towards me with your l. f., placing the h. of the r. into its h. *(Can. does this, instd by the J. D.'s example and whisper if necessary.)* That, my Brother, is the f. r. s. in Freemasonry, and it is in that position the secrets of the Degree are communicated; they consist of a Sn., T. and W., please copy me. *(The W. M. rises and himself takes the Stp. .)* The Sn. is given by p.t.r.h., f.a.t.e.i.t.f.o.a.s., t.t.l.o.t.t.d.i.s.a.a.d.i.t.t.s.; this alludes to the symbolic penalty of the degree, which implied that, as a man of honour, an E. A. Freemason would rather have had his t.c.a. than improperly disclose the secrets of Freemasonry.

*(The J.D. should prompt by example in the Sns. and the Sn. is repeated, starting at "man of honour".)*

*The J.D. lifts the Can.'s Rt. Hd. For the W. M. to take, but does not assist in applying the G. .)*

*(W. M. continues.)* The G. or T. is given b.a.d.p.o.t.t., o.t.f.k.j., o.a.b.r.h.; *(The W. M. applies his G. first.)* this G. when mutually given and received, serves to distinguish a Brother by night as well as by day; it also demands a W.; a W. highly prized amongst Freemasons as a safeguard to their privileges; too much caution,

therefore, cannot be observed in communicating it; it should never be given at length, as you are about to receive it, but always by ls. or ss., to enable you to do which I tell you the W., it is . . . . . . . *(The Can. repeats the W., the W. M. then spells it, and the Can. spells it after him, prompted by the J. D. After this the Can. is not allowed to pronounce the W. in full again.)* As in the course of the ceremony you will be called upon for this W., the J. D. will now dictate the answers you are to give. *(The W. M. maintains the G. .)*

W. M.– What is this?

Can.– *(Prompted aloud by J. D. .)* The G. or T. of an E. A. Freemason.

W. M.– What does this G. demand?

Can.– *(Prompted aloud.)* A.W. .

W. M.– Give me that W. .

Can.– *(Prompted quickly by J. D. to prevent him giving the W. .)* At my initiation I was taught to be cautious, but I will l. or h. it with you.

W. M.– H. it, and begin. *(The full W. is not repeated in full after lg. or hg. .)*

Can.– . . W. M.

W. M.– This W. is derived from the

l.h.p. that stood at the p.e. of K.S.T., so named after . . . . . . , a G. G. of D., a P. and R. in I. . The import of the W. is . . . . . . . . Pass . . . . .

*(The W. M. places the Can.'s Rt. Hd. in the J. D.'s Lt. . It should be noted that the W. M. has retained the Can.'s Hd. throughout the colloquy. The J. D. conducts the Can. to the E. side of the J. W.'s Pedestal, where they face W. , about three feet from it. The J. D. whispers "keep still", releases the Can.'s Hd. , takes the Stp. and shews the Sn. .)*

J.D.– Bro. J. W., I present to you Bro. *(surname)* on his Initiation. *(Cuts Sn. .)*

J.W.– I will thank Bro. *(surname)* to advance to me as an E. A. Freemason, shewing the Sn. *(The J. D. and Can. do this together and the Sn. is cut. .)*

J. W.– Have you anything to communicate?

Can.– *(No Sn. , but prompted by J. D. .)* I have.

*(The J. W. rises. and the J. D. with his Lt. Hd., places the Rt. Hd. of the Can. in that of the J. W. . The J. W. waits until the J. D. has adjusted the Can.'s G., before*

*applying his own. The G. is now retained to the end of the colloquy.)*

J.W.– What is this?

Can.– *(Prompted by J. D. .)* The G. or T. of an E. A. Freemason.

J. W.– What does this G. demand?

Can.– *(Prompted)* A. W. . .

J.W.– Give me that W . . . *(The J.D. prompts quickly to prevent the Can. giving the W. .)*

Can.– At my initiation, I was taught to be cautious, but I will l. or h. it with you.

J.W.– H. it and begin. *(It may be l . . d, but the complete W. is not re-repeated.)*

Can.– . . . . . J. W. . . . . .

J. W.– Pass . . . . *(The J.D. takes the Can.'s Hd. and conducts him to the S. W. in a similar manner.)*

J.D.– *(Releases Can.'s Rt. Hd. , whispers "keep still" and with Stp. and Sn . .)* Bro. S. W., I present to you Bro. *(surname)* on his initiation. *(Cuts Sn. .)*

S. W.– I will thank Bro. *(surname)* to advance to me as an E. A. Freemason. *(The J.D. and the Can. take the Stp. only and wait.)*

S. W.– What is that?

Can.– *(Prompted.)* The f.r.s. in Freemasonry. *(The Stp. is maintained.)*

S. W.– Do you bring anything with you?

Can.– *(Prompted)* I do. *(The J.D. and Can. shew Sn. , which they cut.)*

S. W.– What is that?

Can.– *(Prompted.)* The Sn. of an E. A. Freemason.

S. W.– To what does it allude?

Can.– *(Prompted.)* :–

To the symbolic penalty of the degree, which implied that, as a man of honour, an E. A. Freemason would rather have had his t.c.a. than improperly disclose the secrets of Freemasonry.

*(The Stp. is taken and the Sn. commenced at "as a man of honour".)*

S. W.– Have you anything to communicate?

Can.– *(Prompted.)* I have.

*(The S. W. rises and the J. D. with his Lt. Hd. places the Rt. Hd. of the Can. in that of the S. W. The S. W. waits until the J. D. has adjusted the Can.'s G. before applying his own. The G. is now retained to the end of the colloquy.)*

S. W.– What is this?

Can.– *(Prompted.)* The G. or T. of an E. A. Freemason.

S. W.– What does this G. demand.

Can.– *(Prompted.)* A W.

S. W.– Give me that W. *(J.D. prompts quickly to prevent him giving the W. .)*

Can.– At my Initiation I was taught to be cautious, but I will l. or h. it with you.

S. W.– L. it and begin. *(It may be H. but the complete W. is not repeated.)*

S. W.– Whence is this W. derived?

Can.– *(Prompted.)* From the l.h.p. that stood at the p.e. of K.S.T., so named after . . . . . a G. G. of D., a P. and R. in I.

S. W.– The import of theW.

Can.– *(Prompted)* . . . . . . . .

S. W.– Pass . . . . . . . *(The S. W. remains standing and the Can. is taken past the Pedestal and with a forward left wheel the J. D. places the Can.'s Rt. Hd. in the S. Wdn's Lt. The J. D. arranges the Can. to face E. and stands at his Lt.)*

S. W.– *(With Stp. and Sn. .)* W. M., I present to you Bro. *(full name)* on his Initiation for some mark of your favour. *(S. W. retains Sn. .)*

*(The D. C. takes the B. on a cushion to*

*the W. M., who holds up the B. and addresses the S. W. .)*

W. M.– Bro. S. W., I delegate you to invest our Brother with the distinguishing badge of an E. A. Freemason. *(S. W. cuts Sn. .)*

*(The W. M. replaces the B. on the cushion and the D. C. delivers it to the S. W. The J. D. takes the Can.'s Rt. Hd. and turns him to face the S. W. . . The J. D. may assist the S. W. to tie the B. , and in Lodges where the flap is turned up, the S. W. ties so that it remains so. The S. W. then picks up the lower Rt. Hd. corner with his Lt. Hd. and says:–)*

*S. W. to Can.* – Brother *(full name)* by command of the W. M., I invest you with the distinguishing badge of an E. A. Freemason; it is more ancient than the Golden Fleece, or Roman Eagle, more honourable than the Garter, or any other Order in existence, it being the badge of innocence, and the bond of friendship, and I strongly exhort you ever to wear and consider it as such, and I further inform you, that, if you never disgrace that badge *(The S. W. strikes the B. and all the*

*Brethren simultaneously strike their own Bs. .)*, it will never disgrace you. *(The S. W. sits.)*

*(The J.D. turns the Can. to face E. and stands at his Rt. , does not hold the Can.'s Hd.)*

W. M.– I will add to the observations of our Brother S. W., that you are never to put on that badge should you be about to enter a Lodge, wherein there is a Brother with whom you are at variance, or against whom you entertain feelings of animosity; in such a case it is expected that you will invite him to withdraw, in order to settle your differences amicably, which if happily effected, you may clothe, enter the Lodge, and work with that love and harmony which should at all times characterise Freemasons, but if unfortunately, your differences are of such a nature as not to be so easily adjusted, it were better that one or both of you retire, than that the harmony of the Lodge should be disturbed by your presence.

W. M.– Bro. J.D. *(shews Sn. .)* place our Brother in the N. E. part of the Lodge.

*(The S.D. rises and stands about a yard*

*from the N. E. corner, and the J. D. conducts the Can. to stand beside him. all three facing S. .)*

J.D. to Can.– Lt. Ft. across the L., Rt. Ft. down the L., Hs. together s.a.t.f.a.s. .

## *Charge*

W. M. to Can.– It is customary at the erection of all stately and superb edifices, to lay the first, or foundation stone, at the N. E. corner of the intended building; you, being newly admitted into Freemasonry, are placed in the N. E. part of the Lodge, figuratively to represent that stone, and on the foundation laid this evening may you raise a superstructure, perfect in its parts, and honourable to the builder. You now stand to all appearance a just and upright E. A. Freemason, and I give it to you in terms of strong recommendation ever to continue and act as such; indeed, I shall immediately proceed to put your principles in some measure to the test, by calling upon you to exercise that virtue, which may justly be denominated the distinguishing characteristic of a

Freemason's heart – I mean Charity. I need not here dilate on its excellences, doubtless it has often been felt and practised by you, suffice it to say, it hath the approbation of Heaven and Earth, and like its Sister, Mercy, blesses him who gives, as well as him who receives. In a society so widely extended as that of Freemasonry, whose branches are spread over the four quarters of the globe, it cannot be denied that we have many members of rank and opulence, neither can it be concealed, that, among the thousands that are ranged under its banner, there are some who, from circumstances of unforeseen calamity and misfortune, are reduced to the lowest ebb of poverty and distress. On their behalf it is our usual custom to awaken the feelings of every newly-made Brother, by making such an appeal to his charity as his circumstances in life may fairly warrant; whatever, therefore, you have to give you will deposit with the J. D.; it will be thankfully received and faithfully applied.

*(The J. D. leaves the Can. with the S. D. and stands about a yard in front of him,*

*holding out the open palm of his Rt. Hd. .)*

J. D. to Can.– Have you anything to give in the cause of Charity?

Can.– *(He should be given the opportunity to answer, before being prompted.)*

J. D. to Can.– Were you divested of all money and metallic substances previously to entering the Lodge?

Can.– I was.

J. D. to Can.– Otherwise, would you have given freely?

Can.– I would.

*(The J. D. turns to face the W. M. with Stp. and Sn. .)*

J. D.– W. M., our Brother expresses his willingness but pleads inability, having been deprived of every article of value previously to entering the Lodge. *(Alternatively can be rendered:–)* having been divested of all money and metallic substances previously to entering the Lodge. *(The J. D. cuts Sn. and returns to the Rt. side of the Can. .)*

W. M. to Can.– I congratulate you on the honourable sentiments by which you are actuated, likewise on the inability which, in the present instance, precludes you from gratifying them; believe me my Brother, this trial was not made with a view to sport with your feelings, far be from us any such intention; it was made for three especial reasons; first, as I have already premised, to put your principles to the test; secondly, to evince to the Brethren that you had neither m . . . . . nor m . . . . . s . . . . . about you, for, if you had, the ceremony of your initiation thus far must have been repeated; and thirdly, as a warning to your heart, that should you at any time meet a friend or Brother in distressed circumstances who might solicit your assistance, you will remember the peculiar moments you were received into Freemasonry, p . . r and p . . . s, and cheerfully embrace the opportunity of practising that virtue you now profess to admire.

Please step this way, and I will present to your notice the working tools of an E. A. Freemason.

*(The S. D. resumes his seat; the J. D. conducts the Can. to the front of the W. M.. The I. P. M. should have previously placed the W. Ts.) (W. M. rises.)*

W. M.– They are the 24 in. G., the C. G. and the C.. The 24 in. G. is to measure the work, the C. G. to knock off all superfluities, and the C. to further prepare the stone for the hands of the more experienced workman. But, as we are not operative, but free and accepted, or speculative Masons, we apply these tools to morals. In this sense, the 24 in. G. reminds us of the 24 hours of the day, part to be spent in prayer to Almighty God, part in labour and refreshment, and part in serving a friend or brother in time of need, that not being detrimental to ourselves or connections. The C. G. denotes the force of conscience, which should keep down all vain and unbecoming thoughts that might obtrude during the aforementioned periods, so that our words and actions may ascend unpolluted to the Throne of Grace. The C. points out the advantages of education, by which means alone we are rendered fit members for well organised society.

*(During the explanation, the W. M. should hold out each W. T. in turn for the Can. to see. The W. T's must never be laid*

*on the V. of the S. L. .)*

W. M.– As in the course of the evening you will be called upon for certain fees for your initiation, *(If the fees are already paid, this wording should be suitably modified.)* it is but right that you should know by what authority we act. This is our Charter, or Warrant of Constitution. *(The I. P. M. opens it and hands it to the W. M. .)* It was granted to this Lodge by the Most Worshipful Grand Master in *(Year of issue)*. It is open for your inspection at this or any subsequent Lodge meeting; this is the Book of Constitutions, and these are our By-Laws, both of which I recommend to your serious perusal, as by the one *(Hands the B. of Cons. to the Can. .)* you may learn the duties you owe to the Craft in general, and by the other *(Hands the By-laws.)* to this Lodge in particular. You are now at liberty to retire, in order to restore your personal comforts, and on your return to the Lodge, I shall direct your attention to an Ancient Charge,* founded on the

**This Charge will always be given on the Candidate's return.*

excellences of the Institution and the qualifications of its members.

*(The W. M. may now congratulate the Initiate on becoming a member of our Ancient and Honourable Institution.)* *(W. M. sits.)*

*(The J. D. conducts the Can. to the Lt. of the S. W., relinquishes the hand clasp and directs:–)*

J. D. to Can.– Salute the W. M. as an E. A. Freemason. *(The J. D. prompts by example.)*

*(The I . G. unlocks the door and the Can. retires.)*

End of the Ceremony of Initiation.

*(When the Initiate is ready to return the T. gives one K.; the I. G. rises and with Stp. and Sn. reports.)*

I. G. to J. W.– Bro. J. W., there is a report.

*(The J. W., after a re-assuring nod from the W. M. gives one K.; the I. G. cuts Sn., goes to the door which he opens and receives from the T.:–)*

T. to I. G.– Bro. *(surname)* on his return.

*(The I. G. locks the door and at the Lt. of the S. W. reports with Stp. and Sn. .)*

I. G. to W. M.– W. M., Bro. *(surname)* the Initiate, seeks re-admission.

W. M. to I. G.– Admit him Bro. I. G. . *(I. G. cuts Sn. .)*

*(Both Dns., without command, go to the door, which the I. G. opens, and the J. D. conducts the Initiate to the Lt. of the S. W., all three facing E. . The J. D. directs.)*

J. D. to Initiate.– Salute the W. M. as an E. A. Freemason. *(The Dns. prompt by example.)*

W. M.– Bro. J. D., place our Brother in the centre of the Lodge facing E. . *(The Charge is normally delivered from the E., but should it be given by the S. or J. Wdn., the Deacons and Initiate will face S.; in the centre for the J. W., but on the N. side for the S. W. .)*

*(The Brother delivering the Charge, if other than the W. M., will stand throughout, but although the Rubric calls for a G . . l and standing during a certain passage, the Committee of Universal Ritual suggest that the Charge be given without interruption, to avoid disturbing the Recipient's concentration. It is suggested that having both Ds. to support the*

*Can. during the Charge, presents a more impressive spectacle.)*

## *Charge after Initiation.*

W. M. to Can.– Having passed through the ceremony of your Initiation, I congratulate you on being admitted a Member of our Ancient and Honourable Institution; ancient no doubt it is, having subsisted from time immemorial; and honourable it must be acknowledged to be, as, by a natural tendency, it conduces to make all those so who are obedient to its precepts; indeed, no Institution can boast a more solid foundation than that on which Freemasonry rests, the practice of every moral and social virtue; and to so high an eminence has its credit been advanced, that, in every age, Monarchs themselves have been promoters of the Art, have not thought it derogatory to their dignity to exchange the Sceptre for the Trowel, have participated in our mysteries, and joined in our assemblies.

As a Freemason, I would first recommend to your most serious contemplation the V. of the S. L., charging you to consider it as the unerring standard of truth and justice, and to regulate your actions by the Divine precepts it contains; therein you will be taught the important duties you owe to God, to your neighbour, and to yourself. *(The W. M. sounds the G., and the Brethren rise to order with sn. of Reverence.)* *To God*, by never mentioning His name but with that awe and reverence which are due from the creature to the Creator, by imploring His aid on all your lawful undertakings, and by looking up to Him in every emergency for comfort and support. *(The Brethren resume their seats.)* *To your neighbour*, by acting with him on the square, by rendering him every kind office which justice or mercy may require, by relieving his necessities, soothing his afflictions, and by doing unto him as in similar cases you would wish he should do to you. *And to yourself*, by such a prudent and well-regulated course of discipline as may best conduce to the preservation of your corporeal and mental faculties in their fullest energy, thereby enabling you to exercise those talents wherewith God has blessed you, to His glory and the welfare of your fellow creatures.

As a citizen of the world, I enjoin you to be exemplary in the discharge of your civil duties, by never proposing or at all countenancing, any act which may have a tendency to subvert the peace and good order of society; by paying a due obedience to the laws of any State, which may for a time become the place of your residence, or afford you its protection; and, above all, by never losing sight of the allegiance due to the Sovereign of your native land, ever remembering that nature has implanted in your breast a sacred and indissoluble attachment towards that country, whence you derived your birth and infant nurture.

As an individual, I would further recommend the practice of every domestic as well as public virtue; let Prudence direct you, Temperance chasten you, Fortitude support you, and Justice be the guide of all your actions. Be especially careful to maintain in their fullest splendour those truly Masonic ornaments which have already been amply illustrated, namely, Benevolence and Charity.

Still, as a Freemason, there are other excellences of character to which your attention may be particularly and forcibly directed; among the foremost of these are Secrecy, Fidelity and Obedience. *Secrecy* consists in the inviolable adherence to the Obligation you have entered upon, never improperly to disclose any of those Masonic secrets, which have now been, or may at any future time, be entrusted to your keeping, and cautiously to avoid all occasions which might inadvertently lead you so to do. Your *Fidelity* must be exemplified by a close conformity to the Constitutions of the Fraternity, by adhering to the ancient Landmarks of the Order, by never attempting to extort, or otherwise unduly obtain, the secrets of a superior Degree, and by refraining to recommend any one to a participation in our secrets, unless you have strong grounds to believe that by a similar fidelity he will ultimately reflect honour on our choice. Your *Obedience* must be proved by a strict observance of our laws and regulations; by prompt attention to all signs and summonses; by modest and correct demeanour in the Lodge; by abstaining from every topic of religious or political discussion: by a ready acquiescence in all votes and resolutions duly passed by a majority of the Brethren; and by a perfect submission to the W. M. and his Wardens while acting in the discharge of their respective offices.

And as a last general recommendation, I exhort you to dedicate yourself to such pursuits as may enable you to continue respectable in life, useful to mankind, and an ornament to the society of which you have this day become a member. That you will more especially study such of the liberal arts and sciences as may lie within the compass of your attainment, and that, without neglecting the ordinary duties of your station, you will feel yourself called upon to make a daily advancement in Masonic knowledge.

From the very commendable attention you have given to this charge, I am led to hope that you will duly appreciate the value of Freemasonry and indelibly imprint on your heart the sacred dictates of Truth, of Honour, and of Virtue.

End of the Charge after Initiation.

*(The J. D. turns right and squaring the Lodge returns to his seat at the S. W's. Rt.; the S. D. takes the Initiate's Rt. Hd. and with a Rt. Wheel and squaring the Lodge returns to his seat, the Initiate sitting beside him on his Rt. .)*

*(When the lecture on the 1st Tracing Board is to be given, the Deacons and Initiate remain in the centre and the D. C. places the T. B. in position, in front of the Initiate. The Lecturer may stand either by the N. or S. side; whichever he finds more convenient.)*

## *Explanation of the First Tracing Board.*

The usages and customs among Freemasons have ever borne a near affinity to those of the Ancient Egyptians. Their philosophers, unwilling to expose their mysteries to vulgar eyes, concealed their particular tenets and principles of policy and philosophy under hieroglyphical figures, and expressed their notions of government by signs and symbols, which were communicated to their Priests or Magi alone, who were bound by oath never to reveal them. Pythagoras seems to have established his system on a similar plan, and many others of a more recent date have copied his example. Masonry, however, is not only the most ancient, but the most honourable Institution that ever existed; every character or emblem here depicted serves to inculcate the principles of piety and virtue.

Let me first direct your attention to the form of the Lodge, which is an oblong or parallelopipedon; in length from E. to W., in breadth between N. and S., in depth from the surface of the Earth to the centre, and even as high as the Heavens. A Freemasons' Lodge is described as being of such vast dimensions to shew the universality of the science; likewise that a Freemason's charity should know no bounds save those of prudence.

Our Lodges stand on Holy ground, because the first Lodge was consecrated, and on account of three Grand offerings made on the Holy Mount Moriah, which met with Divine approbation.*[1.] First, the ready compliance of Abraham to the will of God, by not refusing to offer his beloved Son Isaac as a burnt sacrifice, when the Almighty mercifully caused a ram to appear, caught by its horns in a nearby thicket, and which proved a more suitable victim in his stead. Second, the many pious prayers and ejaculations of King David, which appeased the wrath of

God and actually stayed a pestilence then raging among his people, which had been inflicted by the Almighty as a punishment, because the King had disobediently had the tribes numbered. Third, the many thanksgivings, burnt sacrifices, oblations and costly offerings which Solomon, King of Israel made at the completion, consecration and dedication of the Temple at Jerusalem to God's service. These three, did then, do now, and I trust ever will render the groundwork of Freemasonry Holy.

Our Lodges are situated due E. and W. because all places of Divine worship, as well as Freemasons' regular, well-formed, duly constituted Lodges are, or ought to be, so situated; for which we assign three Masonic reasons. First, the Sun, the Glory of the Lord, rises in the E. and sets in the W. Secondly, learning originated in the E., and thence spread its benign influence to the W.*[2.] Thirdly, as the Children of Israel were about to possess the gates of their enemies and inherit the Promised Land, the Almighty was pleased to reveal to them, those three most celebrated institutions, the Moral, Ceremonial and Judicial laws; and for the better solemnization of public worship, as well as a receptacle for the Books and Tables of the Law, Moses caused a Tent or Tabernacle to be erected in the wilderness, which by God's especial command was situated due E. and W.; for Moses did everything according to a pattern shewn him by the Lord on Mount Sinai. This Tent or Tabernacle afterwards proved to be the ground plan, with respect to situation, of that magnificent Temple, built at Jerusalem by that wise and mighty Prince Solomon. This is the third, last and grand reason we Freemasons give, why all places of Divine worship, as well as Freemasons' regular, well-formed and duly constituted Lodges are, or ought to be, so situated.

Our Lodges are supported by three great pillars, which are called Wisdom, Strength and Beauty; Wisdom to contrive, Strength to support, and Beauty to adorn; Wisdom to conduct us in all our undertakings; Strength to support us in all our difficulties, and Beauty to adorn the inward man.*[3.] These three great pillars are emblematical of those three Divine attributes, and further represent S. K. of I., H. K. of T. and H. A. . S. K. of I., for his wisdom in building, completing and dedicating the Temple at Jerusalem to God's service. H. K. of T. for his strength in supporting him with men and materials, and H. A. for his curious and masterly workmanship in beautifying and adorning the same. But as we have no noble orders of Architecture known by the names of Wisdom, Strength and Beauty, we refer them to the three most celebrated, which are the Doric, Ionic and Corinthian. There are in the Lodge, replicas of these three noble orders, supporting lighted candles. By the side of the W. M.'s Pedestal stands one of the Ionic order, representing Wisdom; it is recognised by the spiral scrolls at each corner of the capital. By the S. W.'s Pedestal, stands another of the Doric order, representing Strength and identified by the plain severity of the mouldings. At the J. W.'s Pedestal is a third, of the Corinthian order, representing Beauty; it is distinguished by the clusters of Acanthus leaves and should constantly remind us of the exquisite skill and ability of H. A. .

The covering of a Freemasons' Lodge is a celestial canopy of diverse colours, even the Heavens. The way by which we, as Freemasons, hope to arrive there is by the assistance of a ladder, in Scripture called Jacob's ladder.*[4.] It has many staves or rounds, which point out as many moral virtues, the three principal ones are Faith, Hope and Charity: Faith in the Great Architect of the Universe, Hope in Salvation, and to be in Charity with all men.*[5.] This ladder, which reaches to the Heavens, rests on the V. of the S. L.; because, by the doctrines contained in that Holy Book we are taught to believe in the wise dispensation of Divine Providence, which belief strengthens our Faith, and enables us to ascend the first step; this Faith naturally creates in us a hope of becoming partakers of the blessed promises therein recorded, which Hope enables us to ascend the second step; but the third and last being Charity, comprehends the whole, and the Freemason who is in possession of this virtue in its most ample sense, may justly be deemed to have attained the summit of his profession, figuratively speaking, an ethereal mansion, veiled from mortal eyes by the starry firmament, emblematically depicted in our Lodges by seven stars, which have an allusion to as many regularly made Freemasons, without which number no Lodge is perfect, neither can any Candidate be legally initiated into the Order.

The interior of a Freemasons' Lodge is composed of Ornaments, Furniture and Jewels. The Ornaments are the Mosaic Pavement, the Blazing Star and the Indented or Tesselated Border; the Mosaic Pavement is the beautiful black and white flooring of the Lodge, reminding us of light and darkness, and the joys and sorrows of our chequered existence. The Blazing Star, the Glory in the centre, represents the Sun, the source and giver of all sustenance to life on Earth. The Indented, or Tesselated Border forms the*[6] Skirtwork around the floor of the Lodge and represents the Planets in their endless orbits round the Sun.

The Furniture consists of the V. of the S. L., the Cs. and the S.; the S. Writings are to rule and govern our Faith, on them we obligate our candidates for Freemasonry; so are the Cs. and S., when united, to regulate our lives and actions. The Sacred Writings are derived from God to Man in general, the Cs. belong to the Grand Master in particular, and the S. to the whole Craft.

Of the Jewels, three are movable and three immovable. The movable Jewels are the S., L., and P.; the S. is used by operative masons to try and adjust rectangular corners of buildings, and assist in bringing rude matter into due form; the L. to lay levels and prove horizontals; and the P. to try and adjust uprights while fixing them on their proper bases; they have likewise moral tendencies which will be explained to you in a subsequent Degree.*[7.] They are called movable Jewels, because they are worn by the W. M. and his Wardens, and are transferable to their successors on nights of Installation. The W. M. is distinguished by the S., the S. W. by the L., and the J. W. by the P. *(The W. M. and Wardens should each hold up their Collar Jewels, in turn, for the Lecturer to point them out to the Initiate.)*

The immovable Jewels are the Tracing Board, the Rough and Perfect Ashlars. The Tracing Board is for the Master to lay lines and draw designs on, the Rough Ashlar for the E. A. to carve, mark and indent on, and the Perfect Ashlar for the experienced Craftsman to try and adjust his Jewels on. They are called immovable Jewels because they lie open and immovable in the Lodge for the Brethren to moralise upon.*[8.]

In olden times the Tracing Board in Lodges was quite plain and was actually used for the Master to draw his designs on; these and other emblems, now displayed on present Tracing Boards were drawn directly over the floor of the Lodge, usually by the Tyler in the medium of charcoal and chalk. At the end of the Ceremony the newly admitted apprentice was given a bucket of water and a mop, with orders to erase all traces. But the real Tracing Board of the Lodge; the Spiritual Tracing Board, is that great Book which always lies unfolded during the whole time that the Lodge is open.

In all regular, well-formed and duly constituted Lodges, there is a point within a circle round which the Brethren cannot err; this circle is bounded between N. and S. by two grand parallel lines, the one representing Moses, and the other King Solomon; on the upper part of this circle rests the V. of the S. L. unfolded, supporting Jacob's ladder, and were we as conversant with the doctrines contained in that Holy Book and adherent thereto as those two Grand Parallels were, it would bring us to Him who will not deceive us, neither will he suffer deception. In passing round this circle we must of necessity touch on both those parallel lines, likewise the V. of the S. L., and while a Freemason keeps himself thus circumscribed it is impossible for him to err.

The word Lewis denotes strength, and is here depicted by certain pieces of metal, which, when dovetailed into a stone form a cramp, and enables the operative mason to raise great weights to certain heights with little encumbrance, while fixing them on their proper bases. Lewis likewise denotes the son of a Freemason, whose duty to his parents is to bear the burden and heat of the day, from which they, by reason of their age should be exempt, to assist them in time of need and thereby render the close of their days happy and comfortable. His privilege for so doing, is that of being made a Freemason before any other person, however dignified.

Pendant to the corners of the Lodge are four Tassels, meant to remind us of the four Cardinal Virtues, namely, Temperance, Fortitude, Prudence and Justice,*[9] the whole of which, tradition informs us, were constantly practiced by a majority of our ancient Brethren.

Roman history informs us that the Consul Marcellus built two temples, one dedicated to Virtue and the other to Honour. He constructed them in such a manner, that the only possible means of gaining access to the Temple of Honour was by first passing through the Temple of Virtue; thus leaving an impressive lesson to future ages.

Finally, may Virtue, Honour and

Mercy*[10] be the distinguishing characteristics of every Free and Accepted Mason, till time shall be no more.

*References*

| | | | |
|---|---|---|---|
| *1. | 4th | section, | 1st Lecture |
| *2. | " | " | " " |
| *3. | " | " | " " |
| *4 . | " | " | " " |
| *5. | " | " | " " |
| *6. | 5th | " | " " |
| *7. | " | " | " " |
| *8. | " | " | " " |
| *9. | 6th | " | " " |
| *10. | 7th | " | " " |

End of the Explanation of the first Tracing Board.

THE ENTERED APPRENTICE

## *Ceremony of Closing the Lodge in the First Degree.*

*(The W. M. sounds his G . . l, which is answered by the S. and J. Wardens.)*

W. M.– Brethren, assist in closing the Lodge. *(All rise.)*

W. M.– Bro. J. W., *(Takes Stp. and shews Sn. of E. A. .)* what is the constant care of every Freemason?

J. W.– *(Holding Sn.)* To prove the Lodge close T . d.

W. M.– Direct that duty to be done.

*(The J. W. cuts Sn. .)*

J. W.– Bro. I. G., *(Takes Stp. and shews Sn. .)* prove the Lodge close T . . d.

*(The I. G. cuts Sn., goes to the door, gives knocks of the Degree, and being answered by the T., returns, and with Stp. and Sn. .)*

I. G.– Bro. J. W., the Lodge is close T . . d. *(The I. G. cuts Sn. .)*

J. W.– *(Gives knocks of Degree, takes Stp. and shews Sn. .)* W. M., the Lodge is close T . . d. *(The J. W. cuts Sn. .)*

W. M.– Bro. S. W., *(Takes Stp. and shews Sn. .)* the next care?

S. W.– To see that the Brethren appear to order as Freemasons. *(Cuts Sn. quickly.)*

W. M.– To order, Brethren, as Freemasons. *(All take Stp. and shew the E. A.'s Sn. .)*

W. M.– Bro. S. W., your constant situation in the Lodge?

S. W.– In the W, W. M. .

W. M.– Why are you placed there?

S. W.– As the Sun sets in the W. to close the day, so is the Senior Warden placed in the W. to close the Lodge, by command of the W. M., having seen that every Brother has had his due.

W. M.– Brethren, before the Lodge is closed, *(The Chaplain, if one is appointed, continues with the Prayer.)* Let us with all reverence and humility, express our gratitude to T. G. A. O. T. U., for favours already received; may He continue to preserve the Order, by cementing and adorning it with every moral and social virtue. *(So mote it be, may be sung.)*

W. M.– Bro. S. W., the labours of the evening being ended, you have my command to close the Lodge. *(Gives the knocks of the Degree, using his Lt. Hd. .)*

S. W.– Brethren, in the name of T. G. A. O. T. U., and by command of the W. M., I close the Lodge. *(The W. M., the S. W. and all cut the Sn. . The S. W. gives the knocks of the Degree, using his Rt. Hd., and lowers his c . . . n,; the S. D. attends to the T. B. after the S. W. knocks.)*

J. W.– And it is closed accordingly until the *(Date of next meeting.)* emergencies excepted, of which the Brethren will have due notice. *(The J. W. gives the knocks of the Degree, which is repeated by the I. G. and T.)*

I. P. M.– *(The I. P. M. steps out and closes the V. of the S. L. and lays the S. and Cs. on top.)* Brethren, nothing now remains but, according to Ancient custom, to lock our secrets in a safe and sacred repository. *(Here the I. P. M. places his Rt. Hd. on his Lt. Bt. with Sn. of R. .)* uniting in the act. F. F. F. . *(He gently Sks. his Bt. at each, and the Brethren do likewise.)*

End of the Ceremony of Closing the Lodge in the First Degree.

*(The Closing Ode may now be sung.)*

## *Long Closing.*

You are now about to quit this safe retreat of peace and friendship, and to mix again with the busy world; amidst all its cares and employments, forget not those sacred duties which have been so frequently inculcated, and so strongly recommended in this Lodge: be ye therefore discreet, prudent, and temperate; remember that at this pedestal you have solemnly and voluntarily vowed to relieve and befriend with unhesitating cordiality every Brother who might need your assistance; that you have promised to remind him in the most gentle manner of his failings, and to aid and vindicate his character whenever wrongfully traduced; to suggest the most candid, the most palliating, and the most favourable circumstances, even when his conduct is justly liable to reprehension and blame; thus shall the world see how dearly Freemasons love each other. But, my Brethren, you are expected to extend these noble and generous sentiments still further: let me impress upon your minds, and may it be instilled into your hearts, that every human creature has a just claim on your kind offices; I therefore trust that you will be good to all, more particularly do I recommend to your care the household of the faithful, that by diligence and fidelity in the duties of your respective vocations, liberal beneficence and diffusive charity, by constancy and sincerity in your friendships; a uniformly kind, just, amiable and virtuous deportment, prove to the world the happy and beneficial effects of our ancient and honourable Institution. Let it not be said that you laboured in vain nor wasted your strength for nought – for your work is before the Lord, and your recompense is with God. Finally, Brethren, be of one mind, live in peace, and may the God of love and mercy delight to dwell amongst you, and bless you for evermore.

*(The above, when given precedes the I. P. M.'s security act.)*

*When this examination occurs immediately prior to the Opening, the Challenge should be transferred to the appropriate place before entrusting.*

## *Questions that must be answered by the Candidates before they are Passed to the Second Degree*

*(The Lodge being open in the First Degree, the W. M. G . . ls, and answered by the S. and J. Wdns., proceeds as follows.)*

W. M.– Brethren, Bro. *(surname)*, is this evening a Candidate to be passed to the Second Degree, but it is first necessary he should give proofs of his proficiency in the former, I shall therefore proceed to put the usual questions. *(Any other E. As. may remain in Lodge while the questions are put. The J. D., without command, collects the Can. and conducts him to the Lt. of the S. W. and directs:–)*

J. D. to Can.– Salute the W. M. as an E. A. Freemason. *(The Can. should have been instructed in this, so that on this occasion he can salute without the J. D. prompting by example.)*

W. M. to Can.– Where were you first prepared to be made a Freemason?

Can. – In my heart.

W. M.– Where next?

Can.– In a convenient room adjoining the Lodge.

W. M.– Describe the mode of your preparation.

Can.– I was divested of all ms. and m. ss. and h.w.: my r. a. l. b. and k. were made b.; my r. h. s. d., and a c. t. with a r. n. about my neck.

W. M.– Where were you made a Freemason?

Can.– In the body of a Lodge, just, perfect, and regular.

W. M.– And when?

Can.– When the Sun was at the meridian.

W. M.– In this country Freemasons' Lodges are usually held in the evenings; how do you account for that which at first view appears a paradox?

Can.– The Sun being the centre of our

Solar System, and the earth constantly revolving around it on its axis, and Freemasonry being universally spread over its surface, it necessarily follows that the Sun is always at the meridian with respect to Freemasonry.

W. M.– What is Freemasonry?

Can.– A peculiar system of morality, veiled in allegory, and illustrated by symbols.

W. M.– Name the three grand principles on which the Order is founded.

Can.– Brotherly Love, Relief, and Truth.

W. M.– Who are fit and proper persons to be made Freemasons?

Can.– Just, upright, and free men, of mature age, sound judgment, and strict morals.

W. M.– How do you know yourself to be a Freemason?

Can.– By the regularity of my initiation, repeated trials and approbation, and a willingness at all times to undergo an examination when properly called upon.

W. M.– How do you demonstrate the proof of your being a Freemason to others?

Can.– By Sns., Ts., and the perfect points of entrance.

W. M.– Brethren, these are the usual questions: if any Brother has aught to ask, now is the proper time.

W. M.– Brethren, I must now request all E. As. with the exception of the Can. to retire from the Lodge. *(The E. As. salute and retire, directed by the D. C. . When this is done and the door locked by the I. G., the J. D. conducts the Can. to the front of the W. M.'s Pedestal and they both stand facing E. . )*

W. M. to Can.– Do you pledge your honour as a man and your fidelity as a Freemason, that you will steadily persevere through the Ceremony of being passed to the Second Degree?

Can.– *(Prompted only if necessary)* I do.

W. M.– Do you likewise pledge yourself that you will conceal what I shall now impart to you with the same strict caution as the other secrets in Freemasonry?

Can.– *(Prompted only if necessary.)* I do.

W. M.– Then I will entrust you with a test of merit, which is a P. G. and P. W.

leading to the Degree to which you seek to be admitted *(The W. M. rises and takes the Can.'s Hd. .)* The P. G. is given by a. d. p. o. t. t., b. t. f. a. s. k. j., o. a. b. r. h. . This P. G. demands a P. W., which is ......... *(The Can. repeats.)* ......... denotes ...... and is depicted in a F. C.'s Lodge by an e. of c. near a f. of w.. You must be particularly careful to remember this P. G. and P. W., as without them you cannot gain admission into a Lodge in a superior Degree. Pass ....,.... .

*(The J. D. conducts the Can. to the Lt. of the S. W. and directs.)*

J. D. to Can.– Salute the W. M. as an E. A. Freemason. *(They take the Stp. and do the Sn. together and the Can. retires for preparation.)*

End of the Questions leading from the First to the Second Degree.

***Ceremony of Opening the Lodge in the Second Degree.***

*(The W. M. sounds his G . . l, which is answered by the S. and J. Wdns.)*

W. M.– Bro. J. W., *(Rises, takes Stp. and shews Sn. of 1st. D. .)* are all those present F. C. Freemasons?

J. W.– *(Cuts Sn. .)* Brethren, have you all taken your Second Degree? *(Any E. As. present will stand.)*

J. W.– *(Receiving no reply. Takes Stp. and shews Sn . of 1st. D. . )* W. M. silence implies assent. *(Cuts Sn., but remains standing.)*

*(Alternative reply)* W. M., with the exception of the Bro./Brethren standing, silence implies assent. *(The E. As. salute and retire, directed by the D. C., and the J. W. cuts Sn. and sits while this is done.)*

W. M.– Brethren, assist me to open the Lodge in the Second Degree. *(All rise.)*

W. M.– Bro. J. W., *(Takes Stp. and shews Sn. of 1st. D. .)* what is the first care of every F. C. Freemason?

J. W.– *(Holding Sn. .)* To see that the Lodge is properly T . . d.

W. M.– Direct that duty to be done. *(The J. W. cuts Sn. .)*

J. W.– Bro. I. G., *(The I. G. takes Stp. and shews Sn. of 1st. D. .)* see that the Lodge is properly T . . d. *(The I. G. cuts Sn., goes to the door and gives Knocks of the 1st. D., answered by the T. returns and with Stp. and Sn. of 1st. D. .)*

I. G.– Bro. J. W., the Lodge is properly T . . d. *(Cuts Sn. .)*

J. W.– *(Gives knocks of 1st. D. and with Stp. and Sn. .)* W. M., the Lodge is properly T . . d. *(Cuts Sn. .)*

W. M.– Bro. S. *(The S. W. takes Stp. and shews Sn. of 1st. D. .)* The next care?

S. W.– To see that the Brethren appear to order as Freemasons. *(Quickly cuts Sn. .)*

W. M.– To order, Brethren, as Freemasons. *(All take Stp. and shew Sn. of 1st. D., which they hold.)*

W. M.– Bro. J. W., are you a F. C.

Freemason?

J. W.– I am, W. M., try me and prove me.

W. M.– By what instrument used in Architecture will you be proved?

J. W.– The S. .

W. M.– What is a S. ?

J. W.– An angle of 90 degrees, or the fourth part of a circle.

W. M.– Bro. J. W., you being acquainted with the proper method, will prove the Brethren Craftsmen, and demonstrate that proof to me by copying their example.

J. W.– Brethren, it is the W. M.'s command that you prove yourselves Craftsmen. *(All, with the exception of the W. M. and J. W., cut the 1st. D. Sn., take Stp. and stand to order with the 2nd. D. Sn. .)*

J. W.– *(Seeing all are correct.)* W. M., the Brethren have proved themselves Craftsmen, and in obedience to your command I copy their example. *(The J. W. cuts the 1st D. Sn., takes Stp. and stands to order with 2nd. D. Sn. .)*

W. M.– Bro. J. W., I acknowledge the correctness of the Sn. . *(The W. M. cuts the*

*1st. D. Sn., takes Stp. and stands to order with the 2nd. D. Sn. .)*

W. M.– Brethren, before the Lodge is opened in the Second Degree:– *(Chaplain if appointed.)* Let us supplicate T. G. G. O. T. U., that the rays of Heaven may shed their benign influence, to enlighten us in the paths of virtue and science. *(So mote it be, may be sung.)*

W. M.– Brethren, in the name of T. G. G. O. T. U., I declare the Lodge duly open, *(All drop Lt. Hd. to the side.)* on the S., *(All cut Rt. Hd. .)* for the instruction and improvement of Craftsmen.

*(The W. M. gives Ks. of Second Degree, repeated by the S. and J. Wdns., I. G. and T. at regular intervals. The S. D. crosses the E. and attends to the T. B. . The I. P. M. steps out as the S. D. passes and exposes o. p. of the Cs., salutes and returns. The S. D. should arrange the T. B. immediately the J. W. has given the Ks. .*

*The Brethren all sit after the W. M. has taken his seat.)*

End of the Ceremony of Opening the Lodge in the Second Degree.

## *Special Notes on the Second Degree.*

1. As in the First Degree, it is the responsibility of the Proposer and Seconder to ensure that the Candidate is properly instructed; and in this Degree, particularly in the answers he has to give to the questions before Passing.

   It is very important that they endeavour to explain the meaning and teaching of the First Degree; so that when the S. W. invests the Candidate with the F. C.'s Badge, he can truly say:– "To mark the progress you have made in the Science."
2. The J. D. attends the Candidate whilst the questions are being put, and he must be proficient in them, as it is his duty to prompt the Candidate should he be unable to reply.

3. It is the T.'s duty to prepare the Candidate and he should be sure to fix the A. . with the flap up in those Lodges where this is observed. The T. should also rehearse the Can. in the Stp. and S., and the S. of R. .
4. Before the Opening of the Lodge the D. C. and I. G. should check that each has a large S. to hand and that the F. C. A. . is in a suitable position.
5. When the Lodge has been opened in the Second Degree the I. P. M. should place the W. Ts. ready.
6. The colloquy between the I. G. and T. should be audible to Brethren within the Lodge. Prompting by the S. D. should be aloud when called for in the Ritual and whispered at such other times as may be necessary. All Stps. and Sns. are prompted by example. When both Deacons attend the candidate they should stand slightly behind.
7. The f...s... to be taken are difficult to describe but easy to demonstrate. The S. D. should carefully rehearse them and by constant practice develop the

ability to gauge the distances accurately.

### *Ceremony of Passing to the Second Degree.*

*(The Lodge is opened in the Second Degree and the Can. who must have been examined and entrusted is prepared by the T. . When ready, the T. gives the report in the First Degree.)*

I. G.– *(Advances with Stp. and Second D. Sn. .)* Bro. J. W., there is a report. *(Holds Sn. .)*

J. W.– *(Rises, shews Second D. Sn., but no Kks. .)* W. M., there is a report. *(Holds Sn.)*

W. M.– Bro. J. W., enquire who wants admission. *(J. W. cuts Sn. and sits.)*

J. W.– Bro. I. G., see who seeks admission.

I. G.– *(Cuts Sn., goes to door, which he opens, but remaining within the threshold enquires of the T.:–)* Whom have you there?

T.– *(The colloquy should be audible from within the Lodge.)* Bro. *(full name)*, who has been regularly initiated into Freemasonry, and has made such progress as he hopes will recommend him to be Passed to the Second Degree, for which Ceremony he is properly prepared.

I. G.– How does he hope to obtain the privileges of the Second Degree?

T.– By the help of God, the assistance of the S., and the benefit of the P. G. and P. W. .

I. G.– Is he in possession of the P. G. and P. W. ?

T.– Try him. *(The I. G. takes the Can.'s Rt. Hd. and with the assistance of the T. receives the P. G. and P. W. .)*

I. G.– Wait while I report to the W. M. *(locks door and returns to Lt. of S. W. .)*

I. G.– *(With Stp. and Sn. .)* W. M., Bro. *(full name)*, who has been regularly initiated into Freemasonry, has made such progress as he hopes will recommend him to be Passed to the Second Degree, for which Ceremony he is properly prepared. *(The I. G. should have assured himself that the Can. is properly prepared, during the examination at the door of the Lodge.)*

W. M.– How does he hope to obtain the privileges of the Second Degree?

I. G.– By the help of God, the assistance of the S., and the benefit of a P. G. and P. W. .

W. M.– We acknowledge the propriety of the aid by which he seeks admission; do you, Bro. I. G., vouch that he is in possession of the P. G. and P. W. ?

I. G.– I do. W. M. .

W. M.– Then admit him in due form. *(The I. G. cuts the Sn., which he has held throughout the colloquy.)*

W. M.– *(G . . l, which is repeated by the S. and J. Wdns. .)* Bro. Deacons.

*(The Deacons go to the door, which the I. G. opens; the S. D. takes the Can.'s Rt. Hd. and the I. G. applies the S., which he raises over his head to shew the W. M. that the Can. has been admitted in "due form". The S. D. conducts the Can. to the Lt. of the S. W., the J. D. stands at the Can.'s Lt., the I. G. locks the door.)*

S. D. to Can.– Salute the W. M. as an E. A. Freemason.

*(Both Deacons salute with the Can. and*

*the A. D. C. then places the K . . g S . . l in position.)*

W. M.– Let the Candidate kneel while the blessing of Heaven is invoked in aid of our proceedings. *(G . . l, repeated by S. and J. Wdns., and the Can. is aided to k . . l. The Brethren rise and shew Sn. of R. . The S. D. sees that the Can. shews the Sn. of R. . The Deacons stand slightly behind the Can. with their wands crossed; the S. D.'s in front.)*

PRAYER

*(W. M. or Chaplain. if one appointed.)*

We supplicate the continuance of Thine aid, O merciful Lord, on behalf of ourselves and him who kneels before thee; may the work begun in Thy Name be continued to Thy Glory, and evermore established in us by obedience to Thy Divine precepts. *(So mote it be, may be sung. All disperse Sn. of R., and the Deacons lower their wands.)*

W. M.– Let the Can. rise. *(All sit after the W. M. and the A. D. C. removes the K . . g S . . l. The S. D. takes the Can. by the Rt. Hd., whispering s. o. w. t. l. f. and leads him round the Lodge. the J. D. resumes his seat; on approaching the N. E. corner the S. D. speaks:–)*

S. D. to Can.– Salute the W. M. as an E. A. Freemason in passing. *(The S. D. must release the Can.'s Rt. Hd. and they salute together. The S. D. takes the Can.'s Rt. Hd. and leads him to a position E. of the J. W. .)*

S. D. to Can.– *(Releases Can.'s Rt. Hd. .)* Advance to the J. W. as such, shewing the Sn. and communicating the T. and W. . *(The S. D. prompts by example and the Sn. is cut.)*

J. W.– Have you anything to communicate?

Can.– *(Prompted.)* I have. *(The J. W. rises and takes the Can.'s Rt. Hd. . The S. D. adjusts the Can.'s G. after which the J. W. applies his own.)*

J. W.– What is this?

Can.– *(Prompted.)* The G. or T. of an E. A. Freemason.

J. W.– What does this G. demand?

Can.– A. W. .

J. W.– Give me that W., in this instance freely and at length.

Can.– *(Prompted)* ....

J. W.– Pass .... *(The S. D. receives back the Can.'s Rt. Hd., and leads him on towards the S. W. corner, where he directs:–)*

S. D.– Salute the S. W. as an E. A. F. in passing. *(Releases the Can.'s Rt. Hd. to enable him to do so. At the N. W., by the Lt. of the S. W., the S. D. and the Can. turn Rt. to face E. and wait.)*

W. M.– *(G . . l, repeated by the S. and J. Wdns.)* Brethren, take notice, that Bro. *(full name)* who has been regularly initiated into Freemasonry, is now about to pass in view before you to shew that he is a candidate properly prepared to be Passed to the Second Degree.

*(Whispering s. o. w. t. l. f., the S. D. leads the Can. along the N. and on approaching the N. E. corner speaks:–)*

S. D.– Salute the W. M., again as an E. A. Freemason in passing. *(They salute again together.)*

*(On approaching the J. W. .)*

S. D.– Salute the J. W. as such in passing.

S. D.– *(At Rt. of the S. W. , facing N. .)*

Advance to the S. W. as such shewing the Sn. and communicating the P. G. and P. W. you received from the W. M. previously to leaving the Lodge. *(The S. D. prompts by example and the Sn. is cut.)*

S. W.– Have you anything to communicate?

Can – *(Prompted)* I have.

*(The S. W . rises and takes the Can.'s Rt. Hd. . The S. D. adjusts the Can.'s P. G., after which the S. W. applies his own.)*

S. W.– What is this?

Can.– *(Prompted)* The P. G. leading from the First to the Second Degree.

S. W.– What does this P. G. demand?

Can.– *(Prompted)* A P. W.

S. W.– Give me that P. W.

Can.– *(Prompted)* ......

S. W.– What does ......... denote?

Can.– *(Prompted)* ......

S. W.– And how depicted in a F. C.'s Lodge?

Can.– *(Prompted)* By an e. of c. near a f. of w.

S. W.– Pass ............ *(The S. W. remains standing and the Can. is taken past the Pedestal, without salute, and with a forward Lt. wheel the S. D. places the Can.'s Rt. Hd. in the S. W.'s Lt., the S. D. arranges the Can. to face E. and stands at his Lt. .)*

S. W.– *(Takes Stp. and shews the Sn. of F. .)* W. M., I present to you Bro. *(surname)* a Candidate properly prepared to be Passed to the Second Degree.

W. M.– Bro. S. W., direct the S. D. to instruct the Candidate to advance to the E. by the proper steps. *(The S. W. cuts the Sn., returns the Can.'s Rt. Hd. to the S. D. and sits. The S.D. standing at the Can.'s Rt. slightly turns his head towards the S. W., unobtrusively takes the Stp. and shews Sn. of F. .)*

S. W.– Bro. S. D., it is the W. M.'s command that you instruct the Candidate to advance to the E. by the proper steps. *(Whispering s. o. w. t. l. f., the S. D. conducts the Can. along the N. to about six feet from the N. E. corner, facing S., the J. D. follows and stands at the Can.'s Lt. . The S. D. leaves the Can. in charge of the J. D. and facing the Can. speaks:–)*

S. D. to Can.– The method of advancing from W. to E. in this Degree is by ......... as though ........ a .......... . For your instruction I will first go through them, after which you will please copy me.

*(The S. D. returns to the Rt. of the Can. and speaking aloud demonstrates:–)*

S. D.– Place the feet together, turn out the Rt. Ft., heel to heel, s. a. t. f. a. s., s. o. w. t. l. f....... . *(Having completed the demonstration the S. D. about turns and S . . . g the L. returns, and taking the Can.'s Rt. Hd. speaks and prompts by example:–)*

S. D.– Place your feet together, turn out your Rt. Ft., Heel to Heel. s. a. t. f. a. s., *(whispers)* s. o. w. t. l. f....... . *(The S. D. should have carefully rehearsed these Stps. with a stand-in Can., so that correctly executed, the Can. arrives in the exact position for k . . . g without further movement. At this point the J. D. stands at the Lt. of the Can. .)*

W. M.– As in every degree the secrets of Freemasonry are to be kept separate and distinct, another O. is now required of you, in many respects similar to the former; are you willing to take it?

Can.– *(Prompted only if necessary)*

I am.

W. M.– Then you will kneel on your r. k., place your l. f. so as to form a S., place your r. h. on the V. of the S. L., while your l. a. will be supported in the angle of the S. .

*(The I. P. M. hands the S. to the W. M., who gives it to the J. D. to arrange. The J. D. supports the S. with his Rt. Hd. . The S. D. ensures that the Can.'s r. h. remains on the V. of the S. L. until the W. M. says "Rise duly Ob. ." The W. M. sounds his G . . l, which is answered by the S. and J. Wdns.; the Deacons cross wands with the S. D.'s in front. All rise, and with the exception of the J. D., all shew Sn. of F. .)*

W. M.- State your name at length, and repeat after me.

OBLIGATION

W. M.– I *(full name)*, in the presence of T. G. G. O. T. U., and of this worthy and worshipful Lodge of Fellow Craft Freemasons, regularly held, assembled and properly dedicated, of my own free will and accord, do hereby, *(The W. M. with his Rt. Hd. touches Can.'s Rt. Hd. .)*

and hereon, *(The W. M. with his Rt. Hd. touches the V. of the S. L. .)* solemnly promise and swear, that I will always hele *(heel)*, conceal, and never reveal, any or either of the secrets and mysteries of, or belonging to the Second Degree in Freemasonry, denominated the Fellow Craft, to him who is but an E. A., any more than I would either of them, to the uninitiated or popular world who are not Freemasons. I further solemnly promise to act as a true and faithful Craftsman, to answer Sns., obey Ss., and maintain the principles, inculcated in the former Degree. These several points I solemnly swear to observe, without evasion, equivocation, or mental reservation of any kind.

So help me A. G., and keep me steadfast, in this the S. O. of a F. C. Freemason.

*(The J. D. removes the S. and lowers the Can.'s Lt. Hd. to his side.)*

W. M.– As a pledge of fidelity, and to render what you have repeated a S. O., which might otherwise be considered only as a serious promise, you will seal it with your lips t. . . . on the V. of the S. L.

*(The Can. does this, assisted by S. D. only if necessary. All cut Sn. and the Deacons lower their wands.)*

W. M.– Your progress in Freemasonry is marked by the position of the S. and Cs.; when you were made an E. A. Freemason, b . . p . . of the Cs. were hidden, in this Degree o . . is disclosed, implying that you are now midway in Freemasonry, superior to an E. A., but inferior to that which I trust will hereafter be communicated to you. *(Takes him by the Rt. Hd. .)* Rise, duly obligated F. C. Freemason.

*(The Brethren resume their seats after the W. M. .*

*The S. D. takes the Can. Rt. wheel, and squaring the L. places him at the N. of the W. M. about three feet away facing S. . The J. D. returns to his seat.)*

W. M.– Now that you have taken the S. O. of a F. C. Freemason, I shall proceed to entrust you with the secrets of the Degree. You will therefore advance to me as at your Initiation, shewing the Sn. .

*(The Can. does so, the S. D. prompts by example.)*

You will now take another s. s. towards

me with your Lt. Ft., placing the h. of the Rt. into its h. as before; that my Brother is the s. r. s. in Freemasonry, and it is in that position the secrets of the Degree are communicated. They consist, as in the former, of a Sn., T., and W., with this difference, that in this Degree, the Sn. is of a three-fold nature. Please copy me.

*(The W. M. rises, takes the Stp., facing the Can. .)*

The first part of this three-fold Sn. is called the Sn. of F., and is given by p. t. r. h., w. t. f. a. t. e., i. t. f. o. a. s., o. t. l. b., *(The W. M. illustrates and the S. D. and Can. copy at each stage.)* emblematically to shield the repository of your secrets from the attacks of the insidious. The second part is called the H. Sn. or Sn. of P., and is given by e. t. 1. h., w. t. f. a. t. e., i. t. f. o. a. s. . This took its rise at the time when J. fought the battles of the Lord, for it was in this position he prayed fervently to the Almighty to continue the light of day, until he had completed the overthrow of his enemies. The third is the penal sn. and is given by d. t. 1. h., a. d. t. r. s. a. t. b. a. d. i. t. t. s. a.; this alludes to the symbolic penalty at one time included in the Obligation in this degree which implied that as a man of honour, a F. C. Freemason had he improperly disclosed the secrets entrusted to him would rather have had his l. b. l. o., t. h. t. t. and g. t. t. r. bs. of t. a. or t. d. bts. o. t. f. a. p.

*(In the above, the W. M., the S. D. and Can., repeat the P. Sn. , starting at "man of honour".)*

W. M.– *(continues)* The G. or T. is given by a d. p. o. t. t., o. t. s. k. j., o. a. b. r. h. .

*(The S. D. lifts the Can.'s Rt. Hd. and the W. M. himself applies the G. .)*

This G. also demands a W., a W. to be given and received with the same strict caution as that in the former Degree. It should never be given at length, as you are about to receive it, but always by ls. or ss.; to enable you to do which I will tell you the W., it is . . . . . .

*(The Can. repeats the W. ; then the W. M. spells it and the Can. follows but does not again pronounce the W. in full.)*

As in the course of the Ceremony you will be called on for this W., the S. D. will now dictate the answers you are to give.

W. M.– *(Still holding G.)* What is this?

Can.– *(Audibly prompted)* The G. or T. of a F. C. Freemason.

W. M.– What does this G. demand?

Can.– *(Prompted)* A W.

W. M.– Give me that W.

Can.– *(Prompted quickly by the S. D. .)* In this Degree, as in the former, I was taught to be cautious, but I will 1. or h. it with you.

W. M.– H. *(or l)* it, and begin. *(The W. is not repeated in full after hg. or lg. .)*

Can.– *(Prompted)* ... W. M. ...

W. M.– This W. is derived from the r. h. p. that stood at the p. e. of K. S. T., so named after ......, a P. who officiated at its dedication; the import of the W. is . . ........., and when conjoined with that in the former Degree, ......... , for God said "In ........ will I ......... this mine house to stand firm for ever". Pass ......

*(The W. M. places the Can.'s Rt. Hd. in the S. D.'s Lt., and sits. The S. D. conducts the Can. to the E. of the J. W.'s Ped.; they face W., about three feet away. The S. D. whispers "keep still" and releases the Can.'s Hd. .)*

S. D.– *(With Stp. and Sn. of 2nd. Degree.)* Bro. J. W., I present to you Bro. *(surname)*, on his being Passed to the Second Degree. (S. D. cuts Sn. .)

J. W.– I will thank Bro. *(surname)* to advance to me as a F. C. Freemason, shewing the Sn . . *(The S. D. instructs the Can. by example and whispers if necessary.)*

J. W.– Have you anything to communicate?

Can.– *(Prompted)* I have. *(The J. W. rises and the S. D. adjusts the Can.'s G., after which the J. W. applies his own. The G. is maintained until the end of the colloquy.)*

J. W.– What is this?

Can.– *(Prompted)* The G. or T. of a F. C. Freemason.

J. W.– What does this G. demand?

Can.– *(Prompted)* A W. .

J. W.– Give me that W. .

Can.– *(Prompted quickly to prevent him giving the W. .)* In this Degree, as in the former, I was taught to be cautious, but I will l. or h. it with you.

J. W.– L. *(or h.)* it and begin.

Can.– *(Prompted)* ..... . J. W. ...... .

*(The W. is not repeated after lg or hg. . )*

J. W.– Pass ...... *(The S. D. receives back the Can.'s Rt. Hd. and conducts him to the S. W. similarly.)*

S.D.– *(releases Can.'s Rt. Hd., whispers "keep still" and with Stp. and Sn. of Second Degree.)* Bro. S. W., I present to you Bro. *(surname)* on his being Passed to the Second Degree. *(Cuts Sn. .)*

S. W.– I will thank Bro. *(surname)* to advance to me as a F. C. Freemason, first as an E. A., shewing the Sn. *(The S. D. prompts by example, and together they take the Stp. and go through the First Degree Sn.; they take another Stp. and wait. The S. D. may whisper to prevent the Can. from raising his Hd. to shew Sn. .)*

S. W.– What is that?

Can.– *(Prompted)* The s. r. s. in Freemasonry.

S. W.– Do you bring anything with you?

Can.– *(Prompted)* I do. *(S. D. and Can. shew Sn. of F., which they hold.)*

S. W.– What is that?

Can.– *(Prompted)* The Sn. of F., emblematically to shield the repository of my secrets from the attacks of the insidious.

SW.– Do you bring anything else?

Can.– *(Prompted)* I do. *(Shews H. Sn., still retaining Sn. of F. .)*

S. W.– What is that?

Can.– *(Prompted)* The H. Sn. or Sn. of P. .

S. W.– Whence did it take its rise?

Can.– *(Prompted)* At the time when J., etc., etc. - - - - his enemies.

S. W.– Do you bring anything further?

Can.– *(Prompted)* I do. *(They shew P. Sn. .)*

S. W.– What is that?

Can.– *(Prompted)* The P. Sn. .

S. W.– To what does it allude?

Can.– *(Prompted by word and example.)* The symbolic penalty of this degree, which implied that, as a man of honour, a F.C. Freemason would rather have had his h. t. f. h. b. than improperly disclose the secrets of the degree.

S. W.– Have you anything to communicate?

Can.– *(Prompted)* I have. *(the S. W. rises and the S. D. adjusts the Can.'s G. after which the S. W. applies his own. The G. is maintained until the end of the colloquy.)*

S. W.– What is this?

Can.– *(Prompted)* The G. or T. of a F. C. Freemason.

S. W.– What does this G. demand?

Can.– *(Prompted)* A W. .

S. W.– Give me that W. .

Can.– *(Prompted quickly to prevent him giving the W. . )* In this Degree, as in the former, I was taught to be cautious, but I will l. or h. it with you.

S. W.– H *(or L)* it and begin.

Can.– *(Prompted)* . . . S. W. . . . . . *(The W. is not repeated after hg. or lg.)*

S. W.– Whence is this W. derived?

Can.– *(Prompted)* From the Rt. Hd. P. that stood at the p. e. of K. S. T. so named after ...... a P. who officiated at its dedication.

S. W.– The import of the W. ?

Can.– *(Prompted)* .......... .

S. W.– And what when conjoined with that in the former Degree?

Can.– *(Prompted)* ......... for God said "In ...... will I ........ this mine house to stand firm for ever." *(The S. D. receives back the Can.'s Rt. Hd. .)*

S. W.– Pass ...... *(The S. W. remains standing and the Can. is taken past the Pedestal and with a forward Lt. wheel the S. D. places the Can.'s Rt. Hd. in the S. W's. Lt., the S. D. arranges the Can. to face E. and stands at his Lt. .)*

S. W.– *(Takes Stp. and shews Sn. of F. .)* W. M., I present to you Bro. *(surname)* on his being passed to the Second Degree, for some mark of your favour.

*(S. W. retains Sn. .)*

*(The D. C. takes the F. C. Badge on a cushion to the W. M., who holds up the B. and addresses the S. W. .)*

W. M.– Bro. S. W., I delegate you to invest our Brother with the distinguishing badge of a F. C. Freemason. *(The S. W. cuts Sn. .)*

*(The W. M. replaces the B. on the cushion and the D. C. delivers it to the S. W. . The S. D. takes the Can.'s Rt. Hd. and turns him to face the S. W. . The S. D. may assist the S. W. to tie the B.; in this degree the flap is turned down. The S. W. then picks up the lower Rt. Hd. corner with his Lt. Hd. and says:–)*

S. W. to Can.– Bro. *(surname)*. By command of the W. M., I invest you with the distinguishing badge of a F. C. Freemason, to mark the progress you have made in the science.

*(The S. D. turns the Can. to face E., and stands at his Rt., he does not hold the Can.'s Hd. .)*

W. M.– I will state that the badge with which you have now been invested, points out that as a Craftsman, you are expected to make the liberal arts and sciences your future study, that you may be the better enabled to discharge your duties as a Freemason, and estimate the wonderful works of the Almighty.

W. M.– Bro. S. D., *(Takes Stp. and shews Sn. .)* place our Brother in the S. E. part of the Lodge. *(The S. D. cuts his Sn., and conducts the Can. to the S. E. corner, where he stands at the Can.'s Rt. and directs:–)*

S. D. to Can.– Rt. Ft. across the Lodge, Lt. Ft. down the Lodge; Hs. together, s. a. t. f. a. s. .

## CHARGE

W. M.– Masonry being a progressive science, when you were made an E. A. Freemason, you were placed in the N. E. part of the Lodge, to shew that you were newly admitted; you are now placed in the S. E. part, to mark the progress you have made in the science. You now stand to all appearance a just and upright F. C. Freemason, and I give it to you in terms of strong recommendation ever to continue and act as such, and as I trust the import of the former Charge neither is, nor ever will be, effaced from your memory, I shall content myself with observing, that, as in the former Degree you were made acquainted with the principles of moral truth and virtue, you are now expected to extend your researches into the hidden mysteries of nature and science.

W. M.– Please step this way, and I will present to your notice the working tools of a F. C. Freemason.

*(The S. D. conducts the Can. to the front of the W. M. and stands at his Rt. . The I. P. M. should have previously placed the W. Ts. . ) (W. M. rises)*

W. M.– They are the S., the L., and the P. . The S. is used whilst constructing rectangular corners of buildings, and to assist in bringing rude matter into due form; the L. is to lay l . . . and prove horizontals; and the P. to try, and adjust uprights, whilst fixing them on their proper bases. But as we are not operative, but free and accepted or speculative Masons, we apply these tools to morals. In this sense,* *Here may follow the "Moral Tendencies",* the S. teaches morality, the L. equality, and the P. justness and uprightness of lives and actions. Thus, by S. conduct, L. steps, and upright intentions, we hope to ascend to those blessed mansions whence all goodness emanates.

**Here, the following, known as the "Moral Tendencies" and taken from the 5th. section, 1st. Lecture, may be given as a fuller illustration of the symbolic teaching of the working tools. It is, however, not an obligatory part of the Ceremony.*

*(During the above, the W. M. should hold out each W. T. in turn for the Can. to see. The W. Ts. must never be placed on the V. of the S. L. .) (W. M. sits)*

W. M.– You are now at liberty to retire in order to restore your personal comforts, and on your return to the Lodge, I may call your attention to a lecture on the T. B., should time permit.

*(The S. D. conducts the Can. to the Lt. of the S. W., releases his Hd. and directs; prompting by example.)*

S. D. to Can.– Salute the W. M. as a F. C. Freemason, first as an E. A.

*(The Can. retires, and on his return is admitted in a similar manner to after Initiation, but with the appropriate Sn. . One Deacon only need attend when the Charge and/or the Tracing Board is not to be given.)*

## *The Moral Tendencies*

The S. teaches us to regulate our lives and actions according to Masonic line and rule, and to harmonize our conduct, so as to render us acceptable to that Divine Being from Whom all goodness springs, and to Whom we must give an account of all our actions.

The L. demonstrates that we have all sprung from the same stock, are partakers of the same nature, and sharers in the same hope; and, although distinctions among men are necessary to preserve subordination, yet ought no eminence of situation cause us to forget that we are Brothers, and that he who is on the lowest spoke of fortune's wheel is equally entitled to our regard; for a time will come, and the wisest of us know not how soon, when all distinctions save those of goodness and virtue shall cease, and death, the grand leveller of all human greatness, will reduce us to the same state.

The infallible P., which, like Jacob's ladder, connects heaven and earth, is the criterion of rectitude and truth. It teaches us to walk justly and uprightly before God and man; neither turning to the right nor the left from the strict path of virtue; not to be an enthusiast, persecutor, slanderer or reviler of religion; neither bending towards avarice, injustice, malice, revenge, nor the envy and contempt of mankind, but giving up every selfish consideration which might have a tendency to injure others, to steer the barque of life o'er the rough sea of passion without quitting the helm of rectitude, is the highest perfection to which human nature can attain; and as the builder raises his column by the aid of the level and plumb-rule, so ought every Freemason to conduct himself through life; to observe a due medium between avarice and profusion, to hold the scales of justice with an equi-poise; to make his passions and prejudices coincide with the strict line of his duty, and in all his pursuits to have eternity in view. Thus the S. teaches morality, the L. equality, and the P.

justness and uprightness of life and actions.

*(conclude with)*

So, by S. conduct, L. steps, and upright intentions, we hope to ascend to those blessed mansions whence all goodness emanates.

End of the Ceremony of Passing to the Second Degree.

*(The Charge after Passing and the Tracing Board are delivered with the Candidate standing in the Centre of the Lodge, supported by both Deacons.)*

### *Charge after Passing.*

Having advanced to the Second Degree, we congratulate you on your elevation. It is unnecessary to recapitulate the duties, which, as a Freemason, you are now bound to discharge, or enlarge on the necessity of a strict adherence to them, as your own experience must have established their value. Your past behaviour and regular deportment have merited the honour which we have conferred; and in your new character it is expected that you will not only conform to the principles of the Order, but steadily persevere in the practice of every virtue. The study of the liberal Arts, which tends so effectually to polish and adorn the mind, is earnestly recommended to your consideration, especially the science of Geometry, which is established as the basis of our Art. As the solemnity of our Ceremonies requires a serious deportment, you are to be particularly attentive to your behaviour in our regular assemblies; you are to preserve our ancient usages and customs sacred and inviolable, and induce others, by your example, to hold them in veneration. The laws and regulations of the Order you are strenuously to support and maintain. You are not to palliate or aggravate the offences of your Brethren; but in the decision of every trespass against our rules, judge with candour, admonish with friendship, and reprehend with mercy. As a Craftsman, in our private assemblies you may offer your sentiments and opinions on such subjects as are regularly introduced in the Lecture, under the superintendence of an experienced Master, who will guard the Landmarks against encroachment. By this privilege you may improve your intellectual powers, qualify yourself to become a useful member of society, and, like a skilful Brother, strive to excel in what is good and great. You are to duly honour and obey all regular signs and summonses given and received. You are to encourage industry, and reward merit; supply the wants, and relieve the necessities of Brethren and Fellows, to the utmost of your power and ability; and on no account to wrong them, or see them wronged, but timely to apprise them of approaching danger, and to view their interests as inseparable from your own. Such is the nature of your engagements as a Fellow Craftsman, and these duties you are bound by the most sacred ties to observe.

End of the Charge after Passing.

## *Explanation of the Second Tracing Board.*

When the Temple at Jerusalem was completed by King Solomon, its costliness and splendour became objects of admiration to the surrounding nations, and its fame spread to the remotest parts of the then-known world. There was nothing, however, in connection with this magnificent structure more remarkable, or that more particularly struck the attention, than the two great pillars which were placed at the porchway entrance. That on the ...... was called ......, which denotes in ......; that on the ......, ...... which denotes ......; and when conjoined ......, for God said, "In ...... will I ...... this mine house to stand firm for ever." The height of those pillars was seventeen cubits and a half each, their circumference twelve, their diameter four; they were formed hollow, the better to serve as archives to Masonry, for therein were deposited the constitutional rolls. Being formed hollow, the outer rim or shell was four inches or a hand's breadth in thickness. They were made of molten brass, and were cast in the plains of Jordan, in the clay ground, between Succoth and Zaradatha, where King Solomon ordered those and all his holy vessels to be cast. The superintendent of the casting was H. A. Those pillars were adorned with two chapiters, each five cubits high; the chapiters were enriched with net-work, lily-work, and pomegranates; net-work, from the connection of its meshes, denotes unity; lily-work, from its whiteness, peace; and pomegranates, from the exuberance of their seed, denote plenty. There were two rows of pomegranates on each chapiter, one hundred in a row; those pillars were further adorned with two spherical balls, on which were delineated maps of the celestial and terrestrial globes, pointing out Masonry universal, they were considered finished when the network or canopy was thrown over them. They were set up as a memorial to the Children of Israel of that miraculous pillar of fire and cloud, which had two wonderful effects; the fire gave light to the Israelites during their escape from their Egyptian bondage, and the cloud proved darkness to Pharaoh and his followers when they attempted to overtake them. King Solomon ordered them to be placed at the entrance of the Temple, as the most proper and conspicuous situation for the Children of Israel to have the happy deliverance of their forefathers continually before their eyes, in going to, and returning from, Divine worship.

At the building of K. S. Temple an immense number of artificers were employed; consisting of E. As. and F. Cs. The E. As. received a weekly allowance of corn, wine and oil; the F. Cs. were paid their wages in specie, which they went to receive in the middle chamber of the Temple; they got there by the porchway entrance on the south side. After our ancient Brethren had entered the porch they arrived at the foot of the winding staircase, which led to the middle chamber. Their ascent was opposed by the J. W., who demanded of them the P. G. and P. W. leading from the First to the Second Degree. The P. G. you are all in possession of, and the P. W., you will recollect is..............; ...... denotes ...... , and is here depicted by an e. of c. near a f. of w. The word ...... dates its origin from the time that an army of Ephraimites crossed the river Jordan in a hostile manner against Jephtha, the renowned Gileaditish general; the reason they assigned for this unfriendly visit was, that they had not been called out to partake of the honours of the Ammonitish war, but their true aim was to partake of the rich spoils with which, in consequence of that war, Jephtha and his army were then laden. The Ephraimites had always been considered a clamorous and turbulent people, but they broke out into open violence, and after many severe taunts to the Gileadites in general, threatened to destroy their victorious commander and his house with fire. Jephtha, on his part, tried all lenient means to appease them, but finding these ineffectual, had recourse to rigorous ones; he therefore drew out his army, gave the Ephraimites battle, defeated, and put them to flight, and to render his victory decisive, and to secure himself from like molestation in future, he sent detachments of his army to secure the passages of the river Jordan, over which he knew the insurgents must of necessity attempt to go, in order to regain their own country, giving strict orders to his guards, that if a fugitive came that way, owning himself an Ephtraimite, he should immediately be slain, but if be prevaricated, or said nay, a test W. was to be put to him to pronounce, the W........; they, from a defect in aspiration, peculiar in their dialect, could not pronounce it properly, but called it ........., which small variation discovered their country, and cost them their lives; and Scripture informs us that there fell on that day, on the field of battle and on the banks of the Jordan, forty and two thousand Ephraimites. And as ...... was then a test W. to distinguish friend from foe, K. S. afterwards caused it to be adopted as a P. W .. in a F. C.'s L., to prevent any unqualified person ascending the winding staircase which led to the middle chamber of the Temple.

After our ancient Brethren had given those convincing proofs to the J. W., he said, Pass ......; they then passed up the winding staircase, consisting of three, five, seven or more steps; three rule a Lodge, five hold a Lodge, and seven or more make it perfect; the three who rule a Lodge are the M. and his two Ws.; the five who hold a Lodge are the M., two Ws. and two F . Cs., the seven who make it perfect are two E. As. added to the former five. Three rule a Lodge because there were but three Grand Masters who bore sway at the building of the first Temple at Jerusalem, viz.: S., K. of I., H., K. of T., and H. A.; five hold a Lodge in allusion to the five noble orders of Architecture, viz.: the Tuscan, Doric, Ionic, Corinthian and Composite; seven or more make a perfect Lodge, because King Solomon was seven years and upwards in building, completing, and dedicating the Temple of Jerusalem to God's service; they have likewise a further allusion to the seven liberal arts and sciences, viz.: Grammar, Rhetoric, Logic, Arithmetic, Geometry, Music and Astronomy. After our ancient Brethren had gained the summit of the winding staircase, they arrived at the door of the middle chamber, which they found open, but properly T . . . d against all below the the Degree of a F. C. by the S. W., who demanded of them the Sn., T. and W. of a F. C. After they had given him those convincing proofs, be said: Pass ......; they then passed into the middle chamber of the Temple where they went to receive their wages, which they did without scruple or diffidence; without scruple, well knowing they were justly entitled to them; and without diffidence, from the great reliance they placed on the integrity of their employers in those days. When our ancient Brethren were in the middle chamber of the Temple, their attention was peculiarly drawn to certain Hebrew characters, which are here depicted by the letter G. *(G . . . l, all rise with sn. of F.)* denoting God, the Grand Geometrician of the Universe, to Whom we must all submit, and Whom we ought humbly to adore.

THE FELLOW CRAFT

## *Ceremony of Closing the Lodge in the Second Degree.*

*(The W. M. sounds his G . . l, which is answered by the S. and J. Wdns. .)*

W. M.– Brethren, assist in closing the Lodge in the Second Degree. *(All rise.)*

W. M.– Bro. J. W., *(Takes Stp. and shews Sn. .)* what is the constant care of every F. C. Freemason?

J. W.– To prove the Lodge close T . . d.

W. M.– Direct that duty to be done. *(The J. W. cuts Sn. .)*

J. W.– Bro. I. G., *(The I. G. takes Stp. and shews Sn. .)* prove the Lodge close T . . d.

*(The I . G. cuts Sn., goes to the door and gives knocks of the 2nd. D., and being answered by the T. returns and with Stp. and Sn. reports:–)*

I. G.– Bro. J. W., the Lodge is close T . . d. *(Cuts Sn. .)*

J. W.– *(Gives knocks of D., takes Stp. and shews Sn. .)* W. M., the Lodge is close T . . d. *(Cuts Sn. .)*

W. M.– Bro. S. W., *(Takes Stp. and shews Sn. .)* the next care?

S. W.– To see that the Brethren appear to order as Craftsmen. *(Cuts Sn. quickly.)*

W. M.– To order, Brethren, as Freemasons in the Second Degree. *(All take Stp. and shew Sn., which they hold.)*

W. M.– Bro. J. W., in this position, what have you discovered?

J. W.– The S . . d S . . l. .

W. M.– Bro. S. W., where is it situated?

S. W.– In the c ... e of the b ... g.

W. M.– Bro. J. W., to whom does it allude?

J. W.– To God, T. G. G. O. T. U.

W. M.– Then, Brethren, let us remember that wherever we are, or whatever we do, He is with us, His all-seeing eye observes us, and while we continue to act in conformity with the principles of the Craft, let us not fail to discharge our duty towards him with fervency and zeal. *(So mote it be, may be sung.)*

W. M.– Bro. S. W., the labours of this

Degree being ended, you have my command to close this F. C. Lodge. *(The W. M. gives the 2nd. D. knocks using his Lt. Hd. .)*

S. W.– Brethren, in the name of T. G. G. O. T. U., and by command of the W. M., I close *(Drops Lt. Hd. to the side, and all do likewise.)* this F. C.'s Lodge. *(Cuts Sn. of F. and all copy. The S. W. gives knocks of 2nd. D. using his Rt. Hd. . The S. D. crosses the E., the I. P. M. steps out and conceals b. p. of the cs., salutes as an E. A. and returns. The S. D. attends to the T. B. .)*

J. W.– Happy have we met, happy have we been, happy may we part, and happy meet again; and it is closed accordingly. *(Gives knocks of 2nd. D., which are repeated by the I. G. and T. .)*

*(The Brethren resume their seats after the W. M., and the E. As. are admitted.)*

End of the Ceremony of Closing the Lodge in the Second Degree.

## *Resuming*

*(A Lodge opened in the Second or Third Degree may be resumed in a lower degree by the following method, without going through the full ceremony.)*

W. M.– *(Sounds his G . . l, which is repeated by the S. and J. Wdns. .)* Brethren, by virtue of the power in me vested, I resume the Lodge in the First *(or Second)* Degree.

*(The W. M. gives the knocks of the resumed Degree, which are repeated by the S. and J. Wdns., the I. G., and T. . The S. D. attends to the T. B., and the I. P. M. adjusts the S. and Cs.; he salutes in the new degree and returns.)*

*(A Lodge having been regularly opened in a superior degree and resumed in a lower degree, may be again resumed in the higher degree by the same formula; for*

*instance, a Lodge in the Third Degree having been resumed in the First Degree may again be resumed in the Third Degree.*

*A Lodge once closed in the Second or Third Degree by the full ceremony must not again be resumed in that particular degree.)*

*(Before resuming in a higher degree. the W. M. must be satisfied that all present are qualified. He should G . . l, and repeated by the S. and J. Wdns. speak.)*

W. M.– Brethren. I must now request all F. Cs. *(and / or E. As.)* to retire for the next period of our proceedings.

*(If any are present, they proceed to the Lt. of the S. W., salute in the appropriate degree and retire, under the direction of the D. C. .)*

*(When a Lodge is resumed in a lower degree, the W. M. should remember to give permission for the admission of E. As. or F. Cs. as appropriate. The T. may assist in this by giving a report.)*

*When this examination occurs immediately prior to the Opening, the Challenge should be transferred to the appropriate place before entrusting.*

### ***Questions which must be answered by Candidates before they are Raised to the Third Degree***

*(The Lodge being open in the Second Degree, the W. M. G . . ls, and repeated by the S. and J. Wdns., proceeds as follows:)*

W. M.– Brethren, Bro. *(surname)* is this evening a Candidate to be raised to the Third Degree, but it is first necessary he should give proofs of his proficiency in the former; I shall therefore proceed to put the usual questions. *(Other F. Cs. may remain while the questions are put.)*

*(The S. D., without command, places the Can. at the left of the S. W. and directs:–)*

S.D. to Can.– Salute the W. M. as a F. C. Freemason, first as an E. A. .

*(The Can. should have been instructed in this, so that he can, on this occasion, salute without prompting.)*

W. M. to Can.– How were you prepared to be passed to the Second Degree?

Can.– In a manner somewhat similar to the former, save that in this Degree I was not h. w. my l. a. b. and r. k. were made bare, and my l. h. s. s.

W. M.– On what were you admitted?

Can.– The S.

W. M.– What is a S. ?

Can.– An angle of 90 degrees, or the fourth part of a circle.

W. M.– What are the peculiar objects of research in this Degree?

Can.– The hidden mysteries of nature and science.

W. M.– As it is the hope of reward that sweetens labour, where did our ancient Brethren go to receive their wages?

Can.– Into the middle chamber of K. S. T.

W. M.– How did they receive them?

Can.– Without scruple or diffidence.

W. M.– Why in that particular manner?

Can.– Without scruple, well knowing that they were justly entitled to them, and without diffidence, from the great reliance they placed on the integrity of their employers in those days.

W. M.– What are the names of the two G. Ps. that stood at the p. e. of K. S. T. ?

Can.– That on the ...... was called ......, and that on the ...... ......

W. M.– What are their separate and conjoint significations?

Can.– The former denotes ......, the latter ......, and when conjoined ......, for God said: "In ...... will I ...... this mine house to stand firm for ever."

W. M.– Brethren, these are the usual questions; if any Brother has aught to ask, now is the proper time.

W. M.– Brethren, I must now request all F. Cs., with the exception of Bro. *(surname)* to retire from the Lodge.

*(When this is done, directed by the D. C.; the S. D. conducts the Can. to the front of the W. M.'s Pedestal and they both face E. .)*

W. M. to Can.– Do you pledge your honour as a Freemason, and your fidelity as a Craftsman, that you will steadily persevere through the ceremony of being raised to the Third Degree?

Can.– *(Prompted, only if necessary.)* I do.

W. M.– Do you likewise pledge yourself that you will conceal what I shall now impart to you with the same strict caution as the other secrets in Freemasonry?

Can.– *(Prompted, only if necessary.)* I do.

W. M.– Then I will entrust you with a test of merit, which consists of a P. G. and P. W. leading to the Degree to which you seek to be admitted. *(The W M. rises)* The P.G. is given by a. d. p. w. t. t., b. t. s. a. t. k. j., o. a. b. r. h. . This P. G. demands a P. W., which is . . . . . . . *(Can. repeats)* . . . . . . was the first a . . . r in m . . . . s. The import of the W. is . . . . . . . . . . . . You must be particularly careful to remember this P. G. and P. W., as without them you cannot gain admission into a Lodge in a superior degree.

Pass . . . . . .

*(The S. D. conducts the Can. to the Lt. of the S. W and directs:–)*

S. D. to Can.– Salute the W. M. as a F. C. Freemason, first as an E. A. . *(He retires for preparation.)*

End of the Questions leading from the Second to the Third Degree.

## *Ceremony of Opening the Lodge in the Third Degree.*

*(The W. M. sounds his G . . l, which is answered by the S. and J. Wdns.)*

W. M.– Bro. J. W., *(Rises, takes Stp. and shews Sn. of 2nd. D. .)* are all those present Master Masons?

J. W.– *(Cuts Sn. .)* Brethren, have you all taken your Third Degree? *(Any F. Cs. present will stand.)*

J. W.– *(Receiving no reply, takes Stp. and shews Sn. of 2nd. D. .)* W. M., silence implies assent. *(Cuts Sn., and remains standing.)*

*(Alternative reply.)* W. M., with the exception of the Bro. / Brethren standing, silence implies assent. *(The F. Cs. salute and retire, directed by the D. C., the J. W. cuts Sn. and sits while this is done.)*

W. M.– Brethren, assist me to open the Lodge in the Third Degree. *(All rise.)*

W. M.– Bro. J. W., *(Takes Stp. and shews Sn. of 2nd. D. .)* what is the first care of every Master Mason?

J. W.– To see that the Lodge is properly T . . d.

W. M.– Direct that duty to be done. *(The J. W. cuts Sn. .)*

J. W.– Bro. I. G., *(The I. G. takes Stp. and shews Sn. of 2nd. D. .)* see that the Lodge is properly T . . d *(The I. G. cuts Sn., goes to the door and gives Knocks of the 2nd. D., answered by the T., returns and with Stp. and Sn . of 2nd. D. .)*

I. G.– Bro. J. W., the Lodge is properly T . . d. *(Cuts Sn. .)*

J. W.– *(Gives knocks of 2nd. D. and with Stp. and Sn. .)* W. M., the Lodge is properly T . . d. *(Cuts Sn. .)*

W. M.– Bro. S. W. *(The S. W. takes Stp. and shews Sn. of 2nd. D. .)* the next care?

S. W.– To see that the Brethren appear to order as Craftsmen. *(Quickly cuts Sn. .)*

W. M.– To order, Brethren, as Freemasons in the Second Degree. *(All take Stp. and show Sn. of 2nd. D. which they hold.)*

W. M.– Bro. J. W., are you a Master Mason?

J. W.– I am, W. M., try me and prove me.

W. M.– By what instruments used in Architecture will you be proved?

J. W.– The S. and Cs.

W. M.– You, being acquainted with the proper method, will prove the Craftsmen M. Ms. by Sns., and demonstrate that proof to me by copying their example.

J. W.– Brethren, it is the W. M.'s command that you prove yourselves M. Ms. by Sns. .

*(All, with the exception of the W. M. and J . W., cut Sn., and go through the Sns. of M. M., remaining to order, shewing the R . . y. .)*

J. W.– *(Seeing all are correct.)* W. M., the Craftsmen have proved themselves M. Ms. by Sns., and in obedience to your command, I copy their example.

*(The J. W. cuts Sn., and goes through the Sns. of a M. M., also remaining to order, shewing the R . . y. .)*

W. M.– Bro. J. W., I acknowledge the correctness of the Sns.. *(The W. M. cuts*

*Sn., and goes through the Sns. likewise, remaining to order, shewing the R . . y. .)*

W. M.– Bro. J. W., as a M. M. whence come you?

J. W.– From the E., W. M.

W. M.– Bro. S. W., whither directing your course?

S. W.– Towards the W., W. M.

W. M. to J. W.– What induced you to leave the E. and go to the W. ?

J. W.– To seek for that which is lost, which, by your instruction and our own endeavours, we hope to find.

W. M. to S. W.– What is that which is lost?

S. W.– The genuine secrets of a Master Mason.

W. M. to J. W.– How came they lost?

J. W.– By the untimely death of our M. H. A.

W. M. to S. W.– How do we hope to find them?

S. W.– With the C. .

W. M. to J. W.– What is a C.?

J. W.– A point within a circle, from which every part of the circumference is equi-distant.

W. M. to S. W.– And why with the C.?

S. W.– That being a point from which a M. M. cannot err.

W. M.– Then, Brethren, I will assist you to repair that loss, and may Heaven aid our united endeavours. *(So mote it be, may be sung.)*

W. M.– Brethren, in the name of T. M. H., I declare the Lodge duly open, on the C., for the purpose of Freemasonry in the Third Degree.

*(All drop the R . . y at the word C., but retain the Stp. until after the G. or R. Sn. . The P. Sn. and R . . y are not necessarily repeated at this point. "See Special Notes on Third Degree".*

*The W. M. gives the knocks of the Third Degree, which are repeated by the S. and J. Wdns., the I. G., and T., at regular intervals. The S. D. crosses the E. and attends to the T. B. . The I. P. M. steps out as the S. D. passes and exposes b. ps. of the Cs., salutes with Stp. and P. Sn. with R . . y before returning. The T. B. is changed after the J. W. Kks. .)*

W. M.– To order Brethren, *(All give the G. or R. Sn., exclaiming together:–)*

All Glory to T. M. H. .

*(All sit after the W. M. has taken his seat.)*

End of the Ceremony of Opening the Lodge in the Third Degree.

## *Special Notes on the Third Degree.*

1. As in the previous Degrees, it is still important for the Proposer and Seconder to impart the necessary instruction to the Candidate, so that he has sufficient knowledge of the Second Degree to enable him to answer the questions intelligently and allow the S. W. to say with truth, when investing him: "to mark the further progress you have made in the Science".
2. The S. D. must be proficient in the answers to the questions, in order to prompt the Candidate, should this be necessary.
3. Before the opening of the Lodge, the D. C. is advised to fit the M. M. A., and place it conveniently, thus avoiding disturbance during the Ceremony. He should also make sure that the f.... s....

is to hand, and that the manipulation of the l....... is understood by the Brother concerned. The I. G. should be sure that he has a p... of c.....s. The Wardens should check that their W. Ts. are in place on the Pedestals. Once the Lodge is opened in the Third Degree, the I. P. M. should lay out the W. Ts. of the Degree, ready for the W. M. to present later.

4. The colloquy between the I. G. and T. ought to be audible to the Brethren within the Lodge, and during this examination, the I. G. is responsible to assure himself that the Candidate is correctly prepared; he should not cross over the threshold to do this.
5. The S. D. should have carefully rehearsed the several Stps. and Sns. so that the example to his charge may be immaculate. He should not hesitate to whisper any instructions he may deem necessary.
6. The use of the P. Sn. and the R . . y have not been adequately prescribed in the previous editions of the Universal Ritual Book, and this has undoubtably

led to considerable variation.

The Committee of the Universal Ritual Association have, after much deliberation, arrived at the following interpretation as to the way this Sn. should advisably be used.

The P. Sn. together with the R . . y, is not two Sns. but one, and are regarded as inseparable; except when given "in passing" it is preceded by the Stp. . As in the previous Degrees, it is the rule that the Sn. is shewn while addressing or being addressed by the W. M. or his Wardens; except as otherwise directed in the Rubrics or Ritual.

When the W. M. names a Brother, as for instance, Bro. J. W., the Brother takes the Stp. executes the P. Sn. with the R . . y, which he holds until the end of the discourse; he then merely drops the R . . y.

When an Officer or Brother addresses the W. M., he also takes the Stp. and executes the P. Sn.; standing to order shewing the R . . y until the end of the discourse, when the R . . y is dropped.

When a Brother has to speak at length, as for example, when delivering the Charge after Raising, or when a P. M. is to give the Traditional History and is not invited to occupy the Chair; the P. M. takes the Stp. and executes the P. Sn. with R . . y, which he drops while speaking; at the end of his delivery he again executes the P. Sn., together with a final R . . y.

It is likely that some Lodges will prefer to repeat the P. Sn. with a final R . . y when the W. M. declares the Lodge "duly open on the C.", and also when the S. W. is commanded to close the Lodge in the Third Degree. After a considerable study, the Committee of the Association advise that the repetition is not considered essential. They do emphasise however, that to repeat the P. Sn. without the final R . . y cannot be considered "Universal Practice".

The Full Sns. of a M. M. are used when the Brethren prove themselves M. Ms. by Sns. at the Opening, and are also to be given by Brethren entering the Lodge after it is opened in the Third; always preceded by the E. A. and F. C. Sns. with the Stps. . When retiring or re-entering after temporary retirement, the P. Sn. with the R . . y only is given following the Stp. .

Except when saluting "in passing", Masonic Sns. should not be shewn while moving position in Lodge. This is particularly applicable to the W. M. and the Wdns. during the Closing of the Lodge in the Third Degree.

## *Ceremony of Raising to the Third Degree.*

*(The Can. having been examined, entrusted and retired for preparation, the Lodge is opened in the Third Degree. It is then placed in ........ save a ..... in the E., and the D. C. or Ds. lay down the S..... . Some Lodges may prefer to extinguish the ........ after the I. G. has received the introduction by the T. . When ready, the T. gives the report in the Second Degree.)*

I. G.– *(Rises, takes Stp. and shews P. Sn., holding R . . y.)* Bro. J. W. there is a report. *(Holds R . . y.)*

J. W.– *(Rises, no Kks., takes Stp. and shews P. Sn., holding R . . y.)* W. M., there is a report. *(Holds R . . y.)*

W. M.– Bro. J. W., enquire who wants admission.

J. W.– *(Drops R . . y., and resumes his seat.)* Bro. I. G., see who seeks admission.

*(The I. G. drops R . . y, goes to the door, which he opens and inquires.)*

I. G. to T.– Whom have you there?

T.– *(The following should be audible to Brethren within the Lodge.)* Brother *(full name)* who has been regularly initiated into Freemasonry, Passed to the Degree of a Fellow Craft, and has made such further progress as he hopes will entitle him to be Raised to the Third Degree, for which Ceremony he is properly prepared.

I. G.– How does he hope to obtain the privileges of the Third Degree?

T.– By the help of God, the united aid of the S. and Cs., and the benefit of a P. G. and P. W. .

I. G.– Is he in possession of the P. G. and P. W. ?

T.– Try him. *(The I. G. takes the Can.'s Rt. Hd., and with the assistance of the T., receives the P. G. and P. W. . During the examination the I. G. should observe that the Candidate is correctly prepared.)*

I. G.– Wait, while I report to the W. M. . *(He locks the door and returns to report.)*

I. G.– *(Takes Stp. and shews P. Sn., holding R . . y.)* W. M., Brother *(full name)* who has been regularly initiated into Freemasonry; Passed to the Degree of a Fellow Craft, and has made such further progress as he hopes will entitle him to be Raised to the Third Degree, for which Ceremony he is properly prepared. *(The I. G. holds R . . y.)*

W. M.– How does he hope to obtain the privileges of the Third Degree?

I. G.– By the help of God, the united aid of the S. and Cs., and the benefit of a P. G. and P. W . . *(The I. G. holds R . . y.)*

W. M.– We acknowledge the powerful aid by which he seeks admission, do you Brother I. G. vouch, that he is in possession of the P. G. and P. W. ?

I. G.– I do, W. M. . *(Holds R . . y.)*

W. M.– Admit him in due form. *(The I. G. drops R . . y.; and the W. M. sounds his G . . l, which is repeated by the S. and J. Wdns.)*

W. M.– Brother Deacons.

*(The Ds. go to the door, which the I. G. opens; the S. D. takes the Can.'s Rt. Hd. and the I. G. applies the ...... of the ......... to b. bs. of the Can., and then raises them above his Hd. to shew the W. M. that the*

*Can. has been admitted in "due form". The S. D. then conducts him to the Lt. of the S. W., and the I. G. locks the door. The J. D. stands on the Can.'s Lt., and all three face E. .)*

S. D. to Can.– Salute the W. M. as a F. C. Freemason, first as an E. A. .

*(The Ds. prompt by example and the A. D. C. places the K . . g S . . l in position.)*

W. M.– Let the Candidate kneel while the blessing of Heaven is invoked in aid of our proceedings. *(G . . l, repeated by the S. and J. Wdns. . The Can. kneels.)*

*(All rise and shew the Sn. of R. . The S. D. sees that the Can. also shews the Sn. of R. . Ds. stand slightly behind the kneeling Can. with their wands crossed, the S. D.'s in front.)*

PRAYER

W. M. or Chaplain, *(if one appointed.)*

Almighty and Eternal God, Architect and Ruler of the Universe, at whose creative fiat all things were made, we, the frail creatures of Thy providence humbly implore Thee to pour down on this convocation, assembled in Thy Holy

Name, the continual dew of Thy blessing. More especially we beseech Thee to impart Thy grace to this Thy servant, who now seeks to participate with us in the mysterious secrets of a M. M. . Endue him with such fortitude that in the hour of trial he fail not, but, passing safely under Thy protection through the valley of the shadow of death, he may finally rise from the tomb of transgression, to shine as the stars for ever and ever. *(So mote it be, may be sung. All disperse Sn. .)*

W. M.– Let the Candidate rise.

*(The Ds. lower their wands, the W. M. and Brethren sit, and the A. D. C. removes the K . . g S . . l. . The S. D. takes the Can.'s Rt. Hd., whispers s. o. w. t. l. f., and leads him along the N. . The J. D. resumes his seat.)*

S. D. to Can.– *(On approaching the N. E. .)* Salute the W. M. as an E. A. Freemason in passing. *(The S. D. releases the Can.'s Rt. Hd. and they salute together. The S. D. re-takes the Can.'s Rt. Hd. and leads him to a position E. of the J. W. where he releases the Can.'s Rt. Hd. and instructs:–)*

S. D.– Advance to the J. W. as such, shewing the Sn., *(E. A.)* and communicating the T. and W. *(The S. D. prompts by example and the Sn. is cut.)*

J. W.– Have you anything to communicate?

Can.– *(Prompted)* I have. *(The J. W. rises and takes the Can.'s Rt. Hd. . The S. D. adjusts the Can.'s G., after which the J. W. applies his own.)*

J. W.– What is this? *(The G. is retained.)*

Can.– *(Prompted)* The G. or T. of an E. A. Freemason.

J. W.– What does this G. demand?

Can.– *(Prompted)* A W. .

J. W.– Give me that W., in this instance freely and at length.

Can.– *(Prompted if necessary)* .....

J. W.– Pass ..... *(The S. D. receives back the Can.'s Rt. Hd. and leads him towards the S. W. corner, on approaching it he speaks, releasing Can.'s Hd. .)*

S. D. to Can.– Salute the S. W. as an E. A. Freemason in passing. *(The S. D. retakes the Can.'s Hd. and they again perambulate. On approaching the N. E. the S. D. speaks:–)*

S. D.– Salute the W. M. as a F. C. Freemason in passing. *(The S. D. releases the Can.'s Hd. and they salute together. The Hd. is re-taken and on approaching the J. W. the S. D. speaks, again releasing the Hd. .)*

S. D.– Salute the J. W. as such in passing. *(The Can. is led to a position S. of the S. W., where the Can.'s Hd. is released and the S. D. directs:–)*

S. D.– Advance to the S. W. as such, shewing the Sn. *(F. C.)* and communicating the T. and W. of that Degree. *(The S. D. prompts by example and the Sn. is cut.)*

S. W.– Have you anything to communicate?

Can.– *(Prompted)* I have. *(The S. W. rises and takes the Can.'s Rt. Hd.; the S. D. adjusts the Can.'s G., after which the S. W. applies his own.)*

S. W.– What is this?

Can.– *(Prompted)* The G. or T. of a F. C. Freemason. *(The G. is maintained.)*

S. W.– What does this G. demand?

Can.– *(Prompted)* A. W. .

S. W.– Give me that W., in this instance freely and at length.

Can.– *(Prompted if necessary.)* .......

S. W.– Pass.... . *(The S. W. returns the Can.'s Rt. Hd. to the S. D. and sits.)*

*(The S. D. conducts the Can. to the N. W. corner where they turn Rt. and wait.)*

W. M.– *(G . . l, repeated by S. and J. Wdns. .)* Brethren, take notice, that Bro. *(full name)*, who has been regularly initiated into Freemasonry, passed to the Degree of a Fellow Craft, is now about to pass in view before you to shew that he is a Candidate properly prepared to be Raised to the Third Degree.

*(Whispering s. o. w. t. l. f., the S. D. and Can. again perambulate and on approaching the N. E. the S. D. speaks: and prompts by example.)*

S. D. to Can.– Salute the W. M. again as a F. C. Freemason in passing. *(And on turning the S. E. corner.)* Salute the J. W. as such in passing. *(The Can. is again taken to the position facing N., by the S. W. and the S. D. directs:–)*

S. D.– Advance to the S. W. as such, shewing the Sn. *(F. C.)* and communicating the P. G. and P. W. you received from the W. M. previously to leaving the Lodge.

*(The S. D. prompts by example and the Sn. is cut.)*

S. W.– Have you anything to communicate?

Can.– *(Prompted)* I have. *(The S. W. rises and takes the Can.'s Rt. Hd. . The S. D. adjusts the Can.'s P. G., after which the S. W. applies his own.)*

S. W.– What is this?

Can.– *(Prompted)* The P. G. leading from the Second to the Third Degree.

S. W.– What does this P. G. demand? *(The P. G. is maintained.)*

Can.– *(Prompted)* A P. W. .

S. W.– Give me that P. W. .

Can.– *(Prompted)* ...........

S. W.– What was ........... ?

Can.– *(Prompted)* The first a ..... r in m ...... s.

S. W.– The import of the W. ?

Can.– *(Prompted)* ....... .........

S. W.– Pass ........... *(The S . W. remains standing and the S. D. (without salute) leads the Can. past the S. W.'s Ped.; with a forward Lt. wheel he places the Can.'s Rt. Hd. in the S. W.'s Lt. . He stands at the*

*Can.'s Lt. and they both face E. .)*

S. W.– *(Takes Stp. and shews Sn. of F. .)* W. M. I present to you Bro. *(surname)* a Can. properly prepared to be Raised to the Third Degree. *(Holds Sn. .)*

W. M.– Bro. S. W., direct the S. D. to instruct the Can. to advance to the E. by the proper steps. *(The S. W. cuts Sn., the S. D. takes the Can.'s Rt. Hd. and stands on his Rt., both facing E. . The S. W. sits and the S. D. turns his head towards him, unobtrusively takes the Stp. and shews Sn. of F. .)*

S. W.– Bro. S. D., it is the W. M.'s command that you instruct the Candidate to advance to the E. by the proper steps. *(The S. D. cuts the Sn., and conducts the Can. along the N. to a point level with the H. of the ......; the J. D. follows and stands at the Can.'s Lt. . The S. D. alone goes to the centre and facing the Can. speaks:–)*

S. D. to Can.– The method of advancing from W. to E. in this Degree is by s .... s ...., t... taken as though ......... over an o ... g ...... and f .... b .... or m ........ s .... . For your instruction I will first go through them, after which you will please copy me.

*(The S. D. turns Rt. to face E. .)*

S. D.– Place the feet together; turn out the Lt. Ft., H. to H., s. a. t. f. a. s. - - s. o. w. t. l. f. *(Having completed the demonstration, the S. D. turns Rt. and s .... g the L. returns and takes the Can.'s Rt. Hd., leading him to the centre at the H. of the G. where they stand both facing E. . )*

S. D. to Can.– Place your feet together, turn out your Lt. Ft., H. to H., s. a. t. f. a. s. - - s. o. w. t. l. f. *(The S. D. directs in the 1st. part by indicating with his wand; and prompts by example in the 2nd.)*

*(The S. D. should have carefully rehearsed these steps; so that correctly executed, the Can. arrives in the exact position for k ... g without further movement. At this point the J. D. takes his position at the Can.'s Lt. .)*

W. M. to Can.– It is but fair to inform you that a most serious trial of your fortitude and fidelity, as well as a more S. O. now await you. Are you prepared to meet them as you ought?

Can.– *(Prompted only if necessary.)* I am.

W. M.– Then you will K. on b. ks. . Place b. hs. on the V. of the S. L. .

*(The W. M. sounds his G . . l which is answered by the S. and J. Wdns. . All rise with Sn. of F . . The Deacons cross their wands wth the S. D.'s in front.)*

W. M.– State your name at length, and repeat after me.

OBLIGATION

W. M.– I, *(full name)*, in the presence of T. M. H., and of this worthy and worshipful Lodge of M. Ms., duly constituted, regularly assembled, and properly dedicated, of my own free will and accord, do hereby, *(The W. M. touches the Can.'s Rt. Hd. with his Rt. Hd. .)* and hereon *(The W. M. touches the V. of the S. L. with his Rt. Hd. .)* most solemnly promise and swear, that I will always hele *(heel)*, conceal, and never reveal, any or either of the secrets and mysteries of, or belonging to, the Degree of a M. M. to any one in the world, unless it be to him or them to whom the same may justly and lawfully belong; and not even unto him or them until after due trial, strict examination, and full conviction, that he or they are worthy of that confidence, or in the body of a M. M.'s Lodge, duly opened on the C ... I likewise solemnly engage to adhere to the principles of the S. and Cs., to answer and obey all lawful Sns. and Ss. I may receive from a M. M.'s Lodge if within the length of my c . . t ...; pleading no excuse save sickness, or the pressing emergencies of my public or private avocations. I further solemnly pledge myself to maintain and uphold the F. P. of F. in act as well as in word; that my hand given to a M. M. shall be a sure pledge of brotherhood; that my f . . t shall traverse difficulties and dangers, to unite with his in forming a column for mutual defence and support; that the p .... e of my daily supplications shall remind me of his wants, and dispose my heart to succour his weakness and relieve his necessities, so far as may fairly be done without detriment to myself or connections; that my b . . t shall be the safe repository of his secrets when entrusted to my care – murder, treason, felony, and all other offences contrary to the laws of God and the ordinances of the realm, being at all times most especially excepted; and, finally I will maintain a M. M.'s honour and carefully preserve it as my own; I will not injure him, or knowingly suffer it to be done by others, if in my power to prevent it, but, on the contrary, will boldy repel the slander on his good name, and most strictly respect the honour *(some times rendered "chastity")* of those nearest and dearest to him, in the persons of his wife, his sister, and his child. These several points I solemnly swear to observe, without evasion, equivocation, or mental reservation of any kind. So help me T. M. H., and keep me steadfast, in this, the S. O. of a M. M. .

W. M.– As a pledge of fidelity, and to render what you have repeated a S. O. binding upon you so long as you shall live, you will seal it with your lips t . . . t . . . on the V. of the S. L. .

*(The Can. does this, assisted by the S. D. only if necessary. All drop the Sn. and the Ds. lower their wands.)*

W. M.– Let me once more direct your attention to the position of the S. and Cs.; when you were made an E. A. Freemason, b . . . p . . . of the Cs. were hidden, in the Second Degree o . . . was disclosed, in this the whole is exhibited, implying that you are now at liberty to work with b . . . those p . . . . . . , to render the circle of your Masonic duties complete. *(The W. M. takes him by both Hds. .)* Rise, duly obligated M. M. .

*(The W. M. and Brethren all sit. The Deacons and Candidate step backwards to near the ft. of the g . . . facing E. .)*

## *Charge.*

W. M.– Having taken the S. O. of a M. M., you are now entitled to demand that last and greatest trial, by which means alone you can be admitted to a participation in the secrets of the Third Degree; but it is first my duty to call your attention to a retrospect of those Degrees in Freemasonry through which you have already passed, that you may be the better enabled to distinguish and appreciate the connection of our whole system, and the relative dependence of its several parts. Your admission into Freemasonry in a state of helpless indigence, was an emblematical representation of the entrance of all men on this their mortal existence; it inculcated the useful lessons of natural equality and mutual dependence; it instructed you in the active principles of universal beneficence and charity; to seek the solace of your own distress, by affording relief and consolation to your fellow creatures in the hour of their affliction; but, above all, it taught you to bend with humility and resignation to the will of T. G. A. O. T. U., and to dedicate your heart, thus purified from every baneful and malignant passion, fitted only for the reception of truth and wisdom, to His glory, and the welfare of your fellow creatures.

Proceeding onwards, still guided in your progress by the principles of moral truth, you were led, in the Second Degree, to contemplate the intellectual faculties, and to trace them, in their development, through the paths of Heavenly science, even to the throne of God Himself. The secrets of nature and the principles of intellectual truth were then unveiled to your view. To your mind, thus modelled by virtue and science, nature, however, presents one great and useful lesson more, she prepares you, by contemplation, for the closing hour of your existence, and when by means of that contemplation, has conducted you through the intricate windings of this mortal life, finally instructs you how to die.

Such, my Brother, is the peculiar object of research in this the Third Degree of Freemasonry; it invites you to reflect upon this awful subject, and teaches you to feel that, to the just and virtuous man, death hath no terrors equal to the stains of falsehood and dishonour. Of this great truth the annals of Freemasonry afford us a glorious example, in the unshaken fidelity and noble death of our M., H. A., who was s ... n just before the completion of K. S. T., at the construction of which he was, as you are doubtless aware, the principal architect.

The manner of his death was as follows:–

W. M.– *(G . . l, repeated by S. and J. Wdns.)* Brother Wardens. *(Without shewing Sn., the Wdns. leave their Peds. by the Lt. Hd. sides, taking the necessary W. Ts. with them. The J. W. waits until the S. W. has drawn level with him, and then both advance abreast to the E.; as they come up behind, the Ds. open, one pace outwards, and the Wdns. take their place each side of the Can., the S. W. on the Lt., and the J. W. on the Rt.. The Ds. Rt. about turn and go to the centre, where they attend to the S ....., they then go to the Hd. of the S ....., face each other and cross over; the S. D. passing in front of the J. D.; they return to their seats.*

*The W. M. may consider the following part of the Ceremony more effective if he leaves his Pedestal and stands in front of the Candidate.*

*It is suggested that the custom of c . . . g the Can.'s l . . s for the two first b . . . s is dangerous and untidy; it is advised that the J. W. instructs the Can. to c . . . s his l . . s, Rt. over Lt. after the second b . . w; the W. M. should pause while this is done.)*

W. M.– Fifteen F. Cs. of that superior class of workmen, appointed to preside over the rest, finding the Temple nearly completed, and they not in possession of the secrets of the Third Degree, conspired to obtain them by any means, even having recourse to violence. On the eve, however, of carrying their conspiracy into execution, twelve of the fifteen recanted, but three, of a more determined and atrocious character than the rest, persisted in their impious design, in the prosecution of which they placed themselves respectively at the E., N., and S. entrances of the Temple whither our M. had retired to pay his adoration to T. M. H., as was his wonted custom at the hour of high twelve. Having finished his devotions, our M. attempted to return by the S. entrance, where he was opposed by the first of those ruffians, who, for want of other weapons, had armed himself with a P., and in a threatening manner demanded of our M. the secrets of his exalted Degree, warning him that death would be the consequence of a refusal. Our M., true to his O., replied that those secrets were known to but ...... in the world, and without the consent and cooperation of the other ...... he neither could nor would divulge them, but intimated that he had no doubt patience and industry would, in due time, entitle a worthy Mason to a participation in them, but, for his own part, he would rather suffer death, than betray the sacred trust reposed in him. This answer not proving satisfactory, the ruffian aimed a blow at the h ... of our M., but, being startled by the firmness of his demeanour, it missed his f..., but glanced with sufficient force on his r ... t ... *(here the J. W. touches the Can.'s r ... t ... with the P.)* as to cause him to reel and sink on his l ... k ... Recovering from the shock, our M. made for the N. entrance, where he was accosted by the second ruffian, who received a similar answer to his insolent demand, when the ruffian, who was armed with a L., smote him a blow on the l ... t ... *(here the S. W. touches the Can.'s l ... t ... with the L.)* which brought him to the ground on his r ... k ... Finding all chance of escape cut off at both these points, our M. staggered faint and bleeding to the E. entrance, where the third ruffian was posted, to whom he gave a similar answer with undiminished firmness, for even at this trying moment our M. remained firm and unshaken when the villain, who was armed with a heavy M., struck him a violent blow on the f ..., which laid him ... at his feet *(which the Can. is made to imitate).*

*(The Wdns. see that both the Can.'s Hds.*

*and Ft. are c ..... d, Rt. over Lt. . The Wdns. then stand behind the Can. and the D. C. calls:–)*

D. C.– To order, Brethren. *(All rise and shew the Sn. of R., no Stp., and the Organist plays a few bars of appropriate music, after which:–)*

W. M.– Brethren, take notice, that throughout the recent part of the Ceremony, as well as in his present position, our Brother has been made to represent one of the brightest characters recorded in the annals of Freemasonry, namely:– our M. H. A., who lost his life in consequence of his unshaken fidelity to the sacred trust reposed in him, and I hope this will make a lasting impression on his and your minds, should you ever be placed in a similar state of trial.

D. C.– Brethren, be seated. *(All drop the Sn. of R., and sit, except the Wdns., who also drop the Sn. but remain standing.)*

W. M.– Bro. J. W. *(Takes Stp., shews P. Sn. holding R . . y.)* endeavour to ...... the representative of our M., by the E. A.'s G. .

*(The J. W. drops the R . . y, and passing*

*behind the S. W., K ... s on his Lt. Ke., at the S. side of the Can. to make the T ..... He returns, S ..... g the Lodge, not walking backwards.)*

J . W.– *(holding R . . y.)* W. M., it proves a .... *(Holds R . . y.)*

W. M.– Bro. S. W., *(Takes Stp., shews P. Sn. holding R . . y.)* try that of a F. C. .

*(The S. W. drops the R . . y and proceeds to the S. side of the Can., where he K ... s on his Rt. Ke. to make the T ..... He returns S ..... g the Lodge, passing in front of the J. W. .)*

S. W.– *(Takes Stp., shews P. Sn holding R . . y.)* W. M., it proves a .... likewise. *(Holds R . . y.)*

W. M.– Bro. Wardens, having both failed in your endeavours, there yet remains a third method, which is by taking a firm h ... of the ...... of our Brother's Rt. Hd. and ....... him on the f. p. o. F., of which, with your assistance, I will now make a trial. *(The W dns. drop the R . . y and come forward, to assist the W. M. to ..... the Can. on the f. p. o. F., the J. W. adjusts the Can.'s Lt. Hd. . In this position the W. M. speaks:)*

W. M. to Can.– It is thus, my Brother, that all M. Ms. are ...... from a figurative ..... to a reunion with the companions of their former toil.

*(The W. M. positions the Can. facing S.)*

W. M.– Bro. Wardens, resume your seats.

## *Exhortation*

W. M. to Can.– I will now beg you to observe that the light of a M. M. is but darkness visible, serving only to express that gloom which rests on the prospect of futurity; it is that mysterious veil which the eye of human reason cannot penetrate, unless assisted by that Light which is from above; yet even by this glimmering ray *(points to it)*, you may perceive that you stand on the very brink of the grave, into which you have just figuratively descended, and which, when this transitory life shall have passed away, will receive you into its cold bosom. Let the emblems of mortality which lie before you lead you to contemplate your inevitable destiny, and guide your reflections to that most interesting of all human studies, the knowledge of yourself. Be careful to perform your allotted task while it is yet day, continue to listen to the voice of nature, which bears witness that *(points to his own heart)* even in this perishable frame resides a vital and immortal principle, which inspires a holy confidence that the Lord of Life will enable us to trample the King of Terrors beneath our feet, and lift our eyes to that bright Morning Star, whose rising brings peace and salvation to the faithful and obedient of the human race.

*(Here the W. M. takes the Can. by both Hds. and moves him round to the right until they occupy each other's places, except that the Can is placed almost back to the border, to allow room for further movement. The S. D. crosses and takes his position at the Can.'s Rt.; he prompts by example throughout the following passages, the P. Sn. with R. is repeated at "as a Man of honour".)*

W. M.– I cannot better reward the

attention you have paid to this Exhortation and Charge than by entrusting you with the secrets of this Degree; you will therefore advance to me as a F. C. Freemason, first as an E. A., shewing the Sns. *(Pause while this is done).* You will now take another s. s. towards me with your Lt. Ft., placing the H. of the Rt. into its h., as before; that my Brother, is the t. r. s. in Freemasonry, and it is in that position the secrets of the Degree are communicated; they consist of Sns., a T. and Ws. . Of the Sns., the first and second are casual, and the third p ..... The first casual Sn. is called the Sn. of H., and may be taken from a F. C.'s H. Sn.; you will therefore stand to order as a F. C., and copy me. It is given by lowering t. l. h., f. a. t. e. i. t. f. o. a. s., t. t. l. f. o. t. b. and at the same time p. t. b. o. t. r. h., f. a. t. e. i. t. f. o. a. s., o. t. l. t., slightly i. t. h. o. t. r. s., as though struck with h . . . . . at some d . . . . . . . and a . . . . . . sight. The second casual Sn. is called the Sn. of S., and is given by s. b. t. b. f., and g. s. t. f. w. t. p. o. t. r. h., f. a. t. e. i. t. f. o. a. s. , thus. The P. Sn. is given by p. t. r. h., f. a. t. e. i. t. f. o. a. s. t. t. l. c. o. t. b., d. i. s. a.

and d. i. t. t. s. and r. o. t. c.; this alludes to the symbolic penalty at one time included in the Obligation in this degree which implied that as a man of honour, a M. M. had he improperly disclosed the secrets entrusted to him would rather have been s. i. t. the b. b. t. a. and t. a. s. over t. f. o. e. and w. b. t. f. c. w. o. h., that no trace or remembrance of so vile a wretch may longer be found among men, particularly M. Ms. The G. or T. is the first of the f. p. o. F., which are H. to H., F. to F., K. to K., B. to B., and H. over B., and may thus be briefly explained. H. to H., I greet you as a Brother, and this is the G. of a M. M.; F. to F., I will support you in all your laudable undertakings; K. to K., the posture of my daily supplications shall remind me of your wants; B. to B., your lawful secrets, when entrusted to my care, I will preserve as my own; and H. over B., I will support your character in your absence, as in your presence. It is in this position and then only in a ........, except in open Lodge, that the Ws. of a M. M. are given. They are ......
......

*(The Can. repeats, prompted by the S. D.)*

Both words having a similar import, one signifying the ..... of the B ....... and the other the B ....... is ........ .

W. M.– *(Faces the Can.)* You are now at liberty to retire, in order to restore your personal comforts, and on your return to the Lodge, these casual Sns., T., and Ws., will be further explained, and the Ceremony proceeded with.

*(The W. M. resumes his Chair, and the S. D. conducts the Can. to the Lt. of the S. W. and directs:–)*

S. D. to Can.– Salute the W. M. in the three Degrees, first as an E. A. Freemason.

*(The S. D. prompts by example and the Can. retires. The l ........ is restored and the D. C. or Ds. remove the S ..... When the Can. is ready to return, the T. gives one knock, as for late arrivals, and the I. G. reports; on receiving the J. W.'s signal he opens the door, and receiving the T's announcement locks the door and returns to the Lt. of the S. W. to report.)*

I. G.– *(Takes the Stp., shews the P. Sn.,*

*holding the R . . y)* W. M., Bro. *(surname)* on his return.

W. M.– Admit him, Brother I. G. *(The I. G. drops the R . . y, and the S. D., without command, goes to the door, which the I. G. opens; the S. D. conducts the Can. to the Lt. of the S. W. and directs:–)*

S. D. to Can.– Salute the W. M. as a M. M.; P. Sn. only. *(The S. D. prompts by example, and the R . . y is dropped. The S. W. rises, takes the Can.'s Hd. and takes the Stp., he shews the P. Sn. holding the R . . y and speaks:–)*

S. W.– W. M., I present to you Bro. *(full name)*, on his being Raised to the Third Degree, for some further mark of your favour. *(Holds the R . . y.)*

*(The D. C. takes the B. on a cushion to the W. M., who holds up the B. and addresses the S. W.:–)*

W. M.– Bro. S. W., I delegate you to invest our Brother with the distinguishing badge of a Master Mason. *(The S. W. drops the R . . y.)*

*(The W. M. returns the B. to the cushion, and the D. C. delivers it to the S. W. The S. D. may assist the S. W. to fix the B.*

*which should have been adjusted for size before the Ceremony. It is suggested that the D. C. waits for the discarded F. C. B. before returning.)*

S. W.– Bro. *(full name)*, by command of the W. M., I invest you with the distinguishing badge of a Master Mason, to mark the further progress you have made in the Science.

*(During the foregoing, the S. W. holds the lower Rt. Hd. corner of the B. with his Lt. Hd. . The S. D. then turns the Can. to face E. and stands on his Rt., but does not hold the Can.'s Hd. . The S. W. sits.)*

W. M.– I must state that the badge with which you have now been invested, not only points out your rank as a Master Mason, but is meant to remind you of those great duties you have solemnly engaged to observe, and while it marks your own superiority in the Craft, it calls upon you to afford assistance and instruction to the Brethren in the inferior Degrees.

W. M.– Bro. S. D., *(Takes Stp., shews P. Sn. holding the R . . y.)* place our Brother in the centre of the Lodge.

*(The S. D. drops the R . . y , and conducts the Can.; the J. D. follows and they stand in line facing E., about 12 feet from the W. M. .)*

THE TRADITIONAL HISTORY

W. M.– We left off at that part of our traditional history which mentions the death of our M., H. A.; a loss so important as that of the principal Architect could not fail of being generally and severely felt; the want of those plans and designs, which had hitherto been regularly supplied to the various classes of the workmen, was the first indication that some heavy calamity had befallen our M. The Menatschin, or Prefects, or, more familiarly speaking, the Overseers, deputed some of the most eminent of their number to wait upon King Solomon, and acquaint him with the utter confusion into which the absence of H. A. had plunged them, and to express their apprehension that to some fatal catastrophe must be attributed his sudden and mysterious disappearance. The King's fears being awakened for the safety of his chief artist, he ordered a general muster of the workmen throughout the various departments when three of the Overseers were not to be found. On the same day the twelve who had originally joined in the conspiracy came before the King, and made a voluntary confession of all they knew down to the time of having withdrawn themselves from the number of conspirators. This naturally increased the King's fears; he therefore selected fifteen trusty F. Cs. and ordered them to make a diligent search for the person of our M., if he were yet alive, or had suffered death in any attempt to extort from him the secrets of his exalted Degree. Accordingly, a stated day having been appointed for their return to Jerusalem, they formed themselves into three F. C. Lodges and departed from the three entrances of the Temple. Many days were spent in fruitless search; indeed, one class returned to Jerusalem without having made any discovery of importance: a second, however, were more fortunate, for, on the evening of a certain day, having suffered many privations and much personal fatigue, one of the Brethren, who had rested himself in a reclining posture, to assist his rising, caught hold of a shrub, which, to his surprise, came easily out of the ground. On a closer examination he found that the earth had been recently disturbed; he therefore hailed his companions, and with their assistance opened the ground, and there found the body of our M., very indecently interred. They covered it again with all respect and reverence, and, to distinguish the spot, stuck a sprig of A. at the head of the grave. They then hastened to Jerusalem to impart the afflicting intelligence to King Solomon; who, when the first emotions of his grief had subsided, ordered them to return and raise the body of our M. to such a sepulture as became his exalted rank and superior talents, at the same time informing them, that, by his untimely death, the genuine secrets of a M. M. were lost. He therefore charged them to be particularly careful in observing any casual Sn., T. or W., that might occur while paying this last sad tribute of respect to departed merit. They performed their task with the utmost fidelity, for, on re-opening the ground, one of the Brethren looking round *(W. M. Rises)* observed some of his companions in this position *(gives the sn. of H.)* struck with h ... r at the d ... l and afflicting sight, while others, viewing the g ... y w ... s still visible on his f ..., s ... their own in sympathy with his sufferings. *(Gives the sn. of S. and resumes his seat.)* Two of the Brethren then descended the grave, one of whom endeavoured to raise the body of our M. by the E. A.'s G. which proved a ...; the other tried that of a F. C., which proved a ... likewise; having both failed in their endeavours a more zealous and expert Brother then descended, and taking a ... ... of the ...... of our M.'s r. h., with their assistance, ...... him on the f. p. of F., while others, more animated, exclaimed ...... ......, both words having a similar import, one signifying the d ... of the B ... and the other the B ... is s .... King Solomon ordered that those casual Sns., T. and Ws. should henceforth designate all M. Ms. throughout the universe, until time or circumstances should restore the genuine ones.

It only remains to account for the third class, who, having pursued their researches in the direction of Joppa, were meditating their return to Jerusalem, when, accidentally passing the mouth of a cavern, they heard sounds of deep lamentation and regret; on entering to ascertain the cause, they found three men answering the description of those missing, who, on being charged with the murder, and finding all chance of escape cut off, made a full confession of their guilt. They were then bound and led to Jerusalem, where King Solomon sentenced them to that death which the heinousness of their crime so justly merited.

W. M. (*continues*) – The body of our M. was ordered to be re-interred as near the Sanctum Sanctorum as the Israelitish law would permit. There, in a grave, from the centre three feet E., three feet W., three feet between N. and S., and five feet or more perpendicular. He was not buried in the Sanctum Sanctorum, because nothing common or unclean was allowed to enter there, except the High Priest and he but once a year, and not even then until after many washings and purifications against the great day of atonement for sins, for by the Israelitish law all flesh is deemed unclean. The same fifteen trusty F. Cs. were ordered to attend the funeral clothed in w ... e a ... s and g ... s, as emblems of innocence.

*(The D. C. brings T. B. to W. M.'s Ped. for the explanation and returns it before the Sns. are commenced.)*

## *Explanation of the Third Tracing Board*

The working tools with which our M. was slain were the P ..., L ... and the heavy M. The ornaments of a M. M.'s Lodge are the Porch, Dormer, and Square Pavement. The Porch was the entrance to the Sanctum Sanctorum; the Dormer the window that gave light to the same; and the Square Pavement for the High Priest to walk on. The High Priest's office was to burn incense to the honour and glory of T. M. H., and to pray fervently that the Almighty, of his unbounded wisdom and goodness, would be pleased to bestow peace and prosperity on the Israelitish nation throughout the ensuing year. The three fives allude to the five P. of F., likewise the fifteen trusty F. Cs. The C ....., S ..... and C ......., being emblems of M ..... allude to the untimely death of our M.,

H. A., which occurred three thousand years after the creation of the World. The Sprig of Acacia was placed at the head of his grave.

W. M.– You have already been informed of t ... Sns. in this Degree; the whole are f ..., corresponding in number with the f. p. of F. They are the Sn. of H., the Sn. of S., the P. Sn., the Sn. of G. and D., and the Sn. of J. and E., likewise called the G. or R. Sn. For your instruction I will go through them. Please copy me (*Rises*). This is the Sn. of H., this is the Sn. of S., this the P. Sn.

The Sn. of G. and D. is given by p. t. b. o. t. r. h., f. a. t. e. i. t. f. o. a. s., o. t. r. t., and p. i. s. a. t. f., and d. i. t. t. s., this took its rise at the time our M. staggered faint and bleeding from the N. to the E. entrance of the Temple, when his agony was so great that the perspiration stood in large drops on his f ..... and he made use of this Sn. as a temporary relief to his sufferings. This is the Sn. of J. and E.; it took its rise at the completion of the Temple, when King Solomon with the Princes of his household went to view it; they were so struck with its magnificence and splendour, that with one simultaneous motion they exclaimed, "O wonderful Masons!"

On the Continent of Europe the Sn. of G. and D. is given in a different manner; it is given by i. the fs., and placing the bs. of the hs. to the f., exclaiming: O. c. t. m. a. y. s. o. t. w., on the supposition that all M. Ms. are Brothers to H. A., who was a w.'s son. In Scotland. Ireland and some parts of America it is given in a still different manner, by raising the h.s., the p.s extended towards the h.s, and d. t. w. t. d. m., exclaiming: O. L. my G., O. L. my G., O. L. my G., i. t. n. h. f. t. w's .s. *(W. M. rises)*.

W. M.– Please step this way, I now present to your notice the working tools of a M. M.; they are the S ., P ... and C ... The S ... is an implement which acts on a centre pin, whence a line is drawn to mark out the ground for the foundation of the intended structure; with the P ... the skilful artist delineates the building in a draft or plan, for the guidance and instruction of the workmen; while the C ... enable him, with accuracy and precision, to ascertain and determine the limits and proportions of its several parts. But as we are not operative, but free and accepted, or speculative Masons, we apply these tools to our morals. In this sense the S ... points out that straight and undeviating line of conduct laid down for our pursuit in the V. of the S. L.; the P ... teaches us that our words and actions are observed and recorded by the Almighty Architect, to Whom we must give an account of our conduct through life; while the C ... reminds us of His unerring and impartial justice, in having defined for our instruction the limits of good and evil, and Who will reward, or punish, as we have obeyed or disregarded His Divine commands. Thus the working tools of a M. M. teach us to bear in mind, and act in accordance with, the laws of our Divine Creator, so that when we shall be summoned from this sublunary abode, we may ascend to the Grand Lodge above, where the world's Great Architect lives and reigns for ever.

(N.B.– *The W. M. informs the Can. that*

*he is now entitled to take his seat in a M. M.'s Lodge, and congratulates him.) (W. M. sits).*

*IMPORTANT*

*Attendance at Lodges Overseas*

*See Points of Procedure, Grand Lodge; as published in the Masonic Year Book and also the separate booklet entitled – INFORMATION FOR THE GUIDANCE OF MEMBERS OF THE CRAFT.*

*Brethren should not make any Masonic contact with members of other jurisdictions without first ascertaining from the Grand Secretary's Office at Freemasons' Hall the existence of Regular Masonry in the Country concerned.*

*THE ABOVE SHOULD BE EXPLAINED TO EVERY NEW MASTER MASON.*

End of the Ceremony of Raising to the Third Degree.

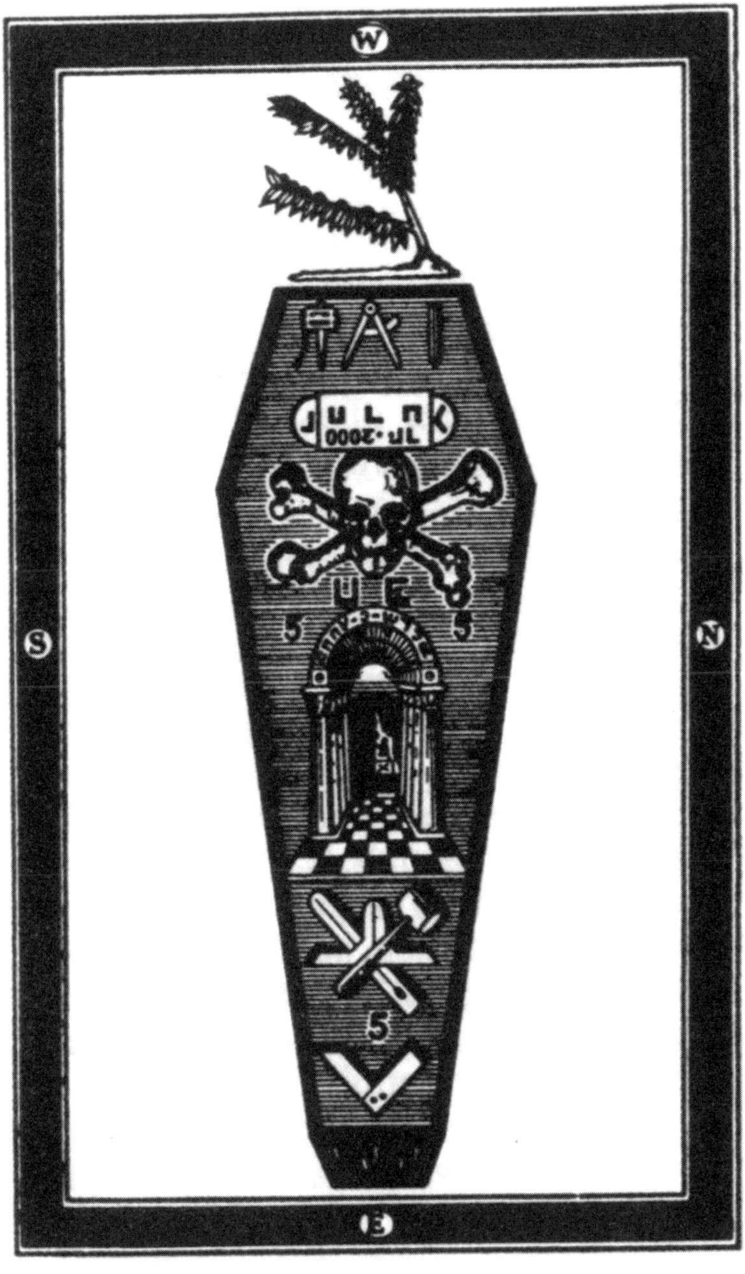


THE MASTER MASON

## Charge after Raising

Brother, your zeal for the Institution of Freemasonry, the progress you have made in the Art, and your conformity to the general regulations, have pointed you out as a proper subject for our favour and esteem.

In the character of a Master Mason, you are henceforth authorized to correct the errors and irregulanties of Brethren and Fellows, and guard them against a breach of fidelity. To improve the morals, and correct the manners of men in society, must be your constant care. With this view, therefore, you are always to recommend to inferiors obedience and submission; to equals, courtesy and affability; and to superiors, kindness and condescension. You are to inculcate universal benevolence, and, by the regularity of your own behaviour, afford the best example for the conduct of others. The Ancient Landmarks of the Order, which are entrusted to your care, you are to preserve sacred and inviolable, and never suffer an infringement of our rites, or a deviation from established usage and custom.

Duty, honour and gratitude now bind you to be faithful to every trust, to support with becoming dignity your new character, and to enforce by example and precept the tenets of the system. Therefore, let no motive cause you to swerve from your duty, violate your vows, or betray your trust; but be true and faithful, and imitate the example of the celebrated Artist whom you have once represented. By this exemplary conduct you will convince the world that merit has been your title to our privileges, and that on you our favours have not been undeservedly bestowed.

End of the Charge.

## *Ceremony of Closing the Lodge in the Third Degree.*

*(The W. M. sounds his G . . l, which is repeated by the S. and J. Wdns. .)*

W. M.– Brethren, assist in closing the Lodge in the Third Degree *(All rise.)*

W. M.– Bro. J. W., *(Takes Stp. shews P. Sn. holding the R . . y.)* what is the constant care of every Master Mason?

J. W.– To prove the Lodge close T . . d.

W. M.– Direct that duty to be done. *(The J. W . drops the R . . y.)*

J. W.– Bro. I. G., *(Takes Stp. shews P. Sn. holding the R . . y.)* prove the Lodge close T . . d.

*(The I. G. drops the R . . y, goes to the door and gives the 3rd. Degree knocks and being answered by the T., returns and with Stp. and P. Sn. holding the R . . y, reports:)*

I. G.– Bro. J. W., the Lodge is close T . . d. *(The I. G. drops the R . . y.)*

J. W.– *(Gives knocks of the Degree, takes Stp. shews P. Sn. holding the R . . y.)* W. M., the Lodge is close T . . d. *(The J. W. drops the R . . y.)*

W. M.– Bro. S. W., *(Takes Stp. shews P. Sn. holding R . . y.)* the next care?

S. W.– To see that the Brethren appear to order as Master Masons.

*(The S. W. drops the R . . y.)*

W. M.– To order, Brethren, as Freemasons in the Third Degree. *(All take Stp. and shew P. Sn. holding the R . . y until the end of the closing.)*

W. M.– Bro. J. W., as a Master Mason, whence come you?

J. W.– From the W., W. M., whither we have been in search of the genuine secrets of a Master Mason.

W. M.– Bro. S. W., have you found them?

S. W.– We have not W. M.; but we bring with us certain substituted secrets which we are anxious to impart for your approbation.

W. M.– Brother Wardens, let those substituted secrets be regularly communicated to me.

*(The Wdns. leave their pedestals by the Lt. Hd. side, temporarily dropping the R . . y, and go to the centre of the Lodge where they face each other about a yard apart, the S. W. facing S. and resume the R . . y. The S. W. has to remember that the secrets are to be communicated to him by the J. W., and await all movements from the latter before responding. The J. W. drops the R . . y and taking a short Stp. shews the Sn. of a F. C.; he then gives the P. G. leading from the 2nd. to the 3rd. Degree, and with their Rt. Hds. raised above their Hds. , the J. W. whispers the P. W. . The J. W. then takes another short Stp. and goes through the full Sns. of a M. M., and on the f. p. o. f. whispers the Ws. . The J. W. then turns Rt. about, and returns to his pedestal, entering from the E. side, where he resumes the R . . y.)*

*(The S. W. then turns to face the W. M., takes the Stp. and shews the P. Sn. holding the R . . y.)*

S. W.– W. M., condescend to receive from me the substituted secrets of a M.M. .

W. M.– Brother S. W., I will receive

them with pleasure, and for the information of the Brethren, you will speak the words aloud.

*(The W. M. leaves his Pedestal by the Lt. Hd. side, temporarily dropping the R . . y, and goes to about a yard in front of the S. W., in the centre of the Lodge, where he resumes the R . . y. The S. W. communicates the secrets as already done by the J. W.; except that he speaks the words aloud. The W. M. then turns Rt. about and returns to his Pedestal, entering from the N. . The S. W. turns Rt. and sq ... g the Lodge, returns to his Pedestal, entering from the S.; they both resume the R . . y.)*

W. M.– Brethren, the substituted secrets of a M. M. having been thus regularly communicated to me, I, as Master of this Lodge, and thereby the humble representative of K. S., do sanction, confirm, and declare, that they shall designate you and all M. Ms. throughout the Universe, until time or circumstances shall restore the genuine ones.

*(The Brethren bending their heads slightly forward, exclaim:–)*

With gratitude to our Master, we bend *(All drop the R . . y, temporarily)*

W. M.– To order, Brethren; All Glory to the M. H. . *(The W. M. and Brethren do this together, and resume the R . . y and maintaining the Stp.)*

W. M.– Bro. S. W., the labours of this Degree being ended, you have my command to close this M. Ms. Lodge.

*(Gives the knocks of the Third Degree, using his Lt. Hd., and holding the R . . y.)*

S. W.– Brethren, in the name of the M. H., and by command of the W. M., I close this M. Ms. Lodge. *(Drops the R . . y. The P. Sn. with final R . . y are not necessarily repeated at this point; as at opening. "See Special Notes on Third Degree".*

*The W. M. and Brethren all follow the S. W.'s example, and he then gives the knocks of the Third Degree, using his Rt. Hd.)*

*(The S. D. crosses the E., the I. P. M. steps out and conceals o . . p .... of the Cs, salutes as a F. C. and returns. The S. D. attends to the T. B. .)*

J. W.– And it is closed accordingly.

*(Gives knocks of the Third Degree, which are repeated by the I. G. and T. . )*

*(The Brethren resume their seats after the W. M., and F. Cs. are admitted.)*

End of the Ceremony of Closing the Lodge in the Third Degree.

***To call the Lodge from Labour to Refreshment.***

*(The W. M. sounds his G . . l, which is answered by the S. and J. Wardens.)*

W. M.– Principal Officers upstanding. *(The three rise.)*

W. M.– Bro. J. W., *(Shews Sn. of D.)*, what time is it?

J. W.– High Time, W. M.

W. M.– Your duty?

J. W.– To call the Brethren from labour to refreshment.

W. M.– I will thank you to discharge that duty.

J.W. *(Cuts Sn.)* – Brethren, it is the W. M.'s command that you cease labour and go to refreshment; keep within hail so as to come on in due time, that profit and pleasure may be the result.

*(The J. W. sounds his G . . l, which is answered by the S. W. and W. M. . The*

*I. P. M. closes the V. of the S. L. without removing: the S. and Cs., but does not salute. The J. W. raises his c . . n and the S. W. lays his down. The S. D. or D. C. attends to the T. B. . The J. W. retains his seat unless excused by the W. M. .)*

***To call the Lodge from Refreshment to Labour.***

*(The W. M. sounds his G . . l. which is answered by the S. and J . Wardens.)*

W. M.– Principal Officers upstanding. *(The three rise.)*

W. M.– Bro. J. W., what time is it?

J. W.– Past high time, W. M.

W. M.– Your duty?

J. W.– To call the Brethren from refreshment to labour.

W. M.– I will thank you to discharge that duty.

J. W.– Brethren, it is the W. M.'s command that you cease refreshment and return to labour, for the further dispatch of Masonic business.

*(He sounds his G . . l, which is answered as before. He lays down his c ... n, and the S. W. raises his. The I. P. M. opens the V. of the S. L. and salutes in the appropriate*

*degree. The S. D. or D. C. attends to the T. B. .)*

*For information regarding "Calling Off", see Points of Procedure; Masonic Year Book.*

## *Installation of Master and Investiture of Officers.*

## *The Ceremony of Installation*

*(With the Lodge open in the First Degree.)*

I. M.– W. Bro. *(name)*, will you please occupy the S. W.'s Chair.

*(The D. C. conducts the W. Bro. to the S. W.'s Ped. . He should not take the Lodge Warden's Collar. The D. C. conducts the retiring Warden to the N. E. . A similar procedure is adopted for the J. W. and I. G. . The W. M. requests the Secretary, D. C. and A. D. C. to continue to act. The W. M. may then request the Officers of his year to line up along the N. side of the Lodge, in order of precedence; when he may say a few words of thanks and appreciation, finally requesting them to pass round so that he can shake each of them by the hand. The A. D. C. should stand at the S. E. corner to receive their*

*collars as they pass to return to their seats.)*

The Lodge is then opened in the Second Degree.

*(The D. C. leads the Master Elect to the centre, about ten feet from the I. M. and holding the M. E.'s Rt. Hd. aloft, takes a short Stp. and shewing the Sn. of F. says:)*

D. C. to I. M.– W. M., I present to you Bro. *(full name)*, Master Elect of this Lodge, to receive at your hands the benefit of Installation.

I. M.– Bro. D. of C., I receive your presentation with much pleasure.

*(The D. C. cuts his Sn. and returns to his seat.)*

*(G . . l, repeated by Wdns.)*

I. M.– Brethren, from time immemorial it has been an established custom among Freemasons for each Lodge once in every year at a stated period to select from its Wardens and Past Wardens a skilled Craftsman to preside over them in the capacity of Master. He must have been regularly elected by the Master, Wardens, and Brethren in open Lodge assembled, and presented to a Board of Installed

Masters to receive from a predecessor the benefit of Installation, the better to qualify him for the discharge of the duties of that important trust. Bro ......, you, having been so elected, I claim your attention while I recite the qualifications which are essential in every candidate for the Master's Chair.

Firstly.– Every candidate for the Office of Master must be of good report, true and trusty, and held in high estimation among his Brethren and Fellows.

Secondly.– He must have been regularly initiated, passed, and raised in the established Degrees of the Order, be well skilled in the noble science, and have duly served the Office of Warden in a regular Lodge.

Thirdly.– He should be exemplary in conduct, courteous in manner, easy of address, steady and firm in principle; well skilled in the Ancient Charges, Regulations, and Landmarks of the Order, able and willing to undertake the management of the work.

Can you, my worthy Brother, accept the Mastership of this Lodge under these qualifications?

M. Elect.– I can W. M.

I. M.– Then I claim your attention while our Bro. Secretary reads from the Book of Constitutions those Charges and Regulations, to all of which your unqualified assent is necessary, which you will signify by the Sn. of F. after each clause, slightly bowing the head in token of submission.

*(The Secretary proceeds to the S. E. where he salutes as a F. C., reads the fifteen Charges from the Book of Constitutions, salutes again as a F. C. and returns.)*

I. M.– Do you submit to and promise to support those Charges and Regulations as Masters have done in all ages?

M. Elect.– I do. W. M. . *(Shews Sn. of F. .)*

I. M.– Then you will please step this way and take a S. O. of Master Elect. *(The M. E. comes forward.)* You will kneel as a F. C. Freemason. *(The M. E. k . . . s and removes his gloves, placing his Rt. Hd. on the V. of the S. L. . It is not necessary to assume the H. Sn. .)*

I. M.– *(Sounds his G . . l, repeated by the S. and J. Wdns. All rise and shew the Sn. of F. .)*

State your name at length, and repeat after me:–

I, *(name)* in the presence of the G. G. O. T. U. and of this Worthy and Worshipful Lodge of F. C. Freemasons, regularly held, assembled, and properly dedicated, do agree to accept the office of Master of this Lodge, and the duties of that high station, zealously, faithfully, and impartially to administer, to the best of my skill and ability, for the ensuing twelve months, and until a successor shall have been duly elected and installed in my stead. I further solemnly promise that I will not, either during my Mastership nor at any time the Lodge may be under my direction, permit or suffer any deviation from the Ancient Customs and established Landmarks of the Order. I will not administer, or cause to be administered any rite or ceremony contrary to or subversive of our ancient Institution, but will maintain and uphold pure and unsullied the genuine principles and tenets of the Craft. I will observe and to the utmost of my power enforce, a due obedience to those Charges and Regulations to which I have already given my assent, and in every respect conscientiously discharge my duties as a Ruler in the Craft and Master of this Lodge. So help me ... and keep me steadfast in this, the S. O. of Master Elect.

As a pledge of fidelity, and to render what you have repeated a S. O., you will seal it t ... with your lips on the V. of the S. L.

Rise, duly obligated, Master Elect.

*(All dis. Sn. and sit, after the I. M. . The M. E. proceeds to a seat in the S. E. .)*

The Lodge is opened in the Third Degree.

I. M.– Brethren, I must now request all below the rank of Installed Master to retire for the next part of the Ceremony. *(They do so without salutes.)*

*(Here follows the Esotery of the Board of Installed Masters. As the M. E. will be required to invest the I. P. M., he should have received instruction in this from one of the P. Ms. .)*

*(If the Lodge is "Called Off" at the end of the Inner Working, precautions should be taken to ensure that all present are qualified before "Calling On". For information regarding "Calling Off", see "Points of Procedure"; Masonic Year Book.)*

I. M.– Bro. I. G., *(Takes Stp. shews P. Sn. holding the R . . y.)* admit all M. Ms.

*(The I. G. drops the R . . y, and with the assistance of the T. endeavours to get the visiting M. Ms. into the Lodge, after which the M. Ms. of the Lodge enter, and without salutes, line up along the N. side. The D. C. selects a limited number, according to the size of the room, and the remainder go to their seats. The I. G. locks the door, and the lined up Brethren face S.; the D. C. at the Hd. of the line.)*

I. G.– *(Takes Stp. shews P. Sn. holding R . . y.)* Bro. I. M., all M. Ms admitted. *(The I. G. drops the R . . y.)*

I. M.– *(At the Lt. of the W. M. .)* Brethren, during your temporary absence our highly esteemed Brother, *(full name)*, has been duly installed in the Chair of K. S., according to Ancient custom, and I call upon you to salute him as M. Ms. in passing, following and copying our Brother, the D. of C . . . s.

*(After perambulating, the D. C. should halt a little short of the N. E. corner, to allow space for the F. Cs. to come in later, all face S. .)*

I. M.– Brethren, for the first time, in the E., I proclaim Brother *(full name)* W. M. of the ..... .... Lodge, Number ......... on the Register of the Grand Lodge of England, for the ensuing twelve months, and until a successor shall have been duly elected and installed in his stead, and I call upon you to greet him as M. Ms. with three, taking your time from our Brother, the D. of C . . . s.

*(The D. C. crosses to the S. E., and facing the lined up Brethren, speaks:–)*

D. C.– Half left turn, Brethren; G. or R. Sn., three times.

*(The D. C. gives the greeting and the Brethren copy him.)*

D. C.– Half right turn, Brethren.

I. M.– W. M., I will now present to you the W. Ts. of a M. M., which are the S., the P., and the Cs. You are so well acquainted with their use that I need not take up your time or that of the Lodge by explaining them at length. You will therefore close the Lodge in this Degree or resume it in the Second. *(When this is done, the W. Ts. are changed and the I. M. speaks.)*

I. M.– Bro. I. G., *(Takes Stp., shews F. C. Sn. .)* admit all F. C. Freemasons. *(The F. Cs. enter, without salutes, and take a position at the head of the lined up Brethren, next to the D. C. .)*

I. G.– *(Takes Stp. and with F. C. sn. .)* Bro. I. M. all F. Cs. admitted.

I. M.– *(At the Lt. of the W. M. .)* Brethren, during your temporary absence our highly esteemed Brother *(full name)* has been duly installed in the Chair of K. S. according to Ancient custom, and I call upon you to salute him as F. Cs. in passing, following and copying our Brother, the D. of C . . . s. *(At the end of the perambulation the D. C. halts a little before the N. E. corner to allow for the E. As, later. The I. M. follows round behind the Brethren and takes his position at the Lt. of the S. W. .)*

I. M.– Brethren, for the second time, and in the W., I proclaim Brother *(full name)* W. M. of the ......... Lodge, Number ....... on the Register of the Grand Lodge of England, for the ensuing twelve months and until a successor shall have been duly elected and installed in his stead, and I call upon you to greet him as F. Cs. with five, taking your time from our Brother the D. of C . . . s.

*(The D. C. crosses to the S. E., and faces the lined up Brethren.)*

D. C.– Half left turn Brethren; the salutation in this Degree is B., H., B., five times, to the rhythm of the F. C. knocks. Stand to order thus.

*(The D. C. demonstrates once and they all give the greeting following his lead.)*

D. C.– Half right turn, Brethren. *(The I. M. returns to the Lt. of the W. M. .)*

I. M.– W. M., I now present to you the W. Ts. of a F. C. Freemason, which are the S., the L., and the P. . You are so well acquainted with their use also that I will not take up your time or that of the Lodge by explaining them at length. You will therefore close the Lodge in this Degree or resume it in the First. *(When this is done, the W. Ts. are changed and the I. P. M. speaks.)*

I. M.– Bro. I. G., *(Takes Stp. and with E. A. Sn. .)* admit all E. A. Freemasons. *(The E. As. enter, without salutes and take a position at the head of the lined up Brethren, next to the D. C. .)*

I. G.– *(Takes Stp. and with E. A. Sn. .)* Bro. I. M., all E. As. admitted.

I. M.– Brethren, during your temporary absence our highly esteemed Brother *(full name)* has been duly installed in the Chair of K. S. according to Ancient custom, and I call upon you to salute him as E. As. in passing, following and copying our Brother, the D. of C . . . s. *(The I. M. follows round behind the Brethren to a position at the left of the J. W. .)*

I. M.– Brethren, for the third time, and in the S., I proclaim Brother *(full name)* W. M. of the ....... Lodge, Number ....... on the Register of the Grand Lodge of England, for the ensuing twelve months, and until a successor shall have been duly elected and installed in his stead, and I call upon you to greet him as E. As. with three, taking your time from our Brother, the D. of C . . . s.

*(The D. C. crosses to the S. E. .)*

D. C.– Half left turn, Brethren; E. A.'s Sn., three times. *(The D. C. gives the greeting and the Brethren copy his example. The I. M. returns to Lt. of W. M. .)*

I. M.– W. M., I now present to you the W. Ts. of an E. A. Freemason, which are the 24 in. G., the C. G., and the C. . You are so well acquainted with their use likewise that I will not take up your time or that of the Lodge by explaining them at length.

I. M.– *(to lined up Brethren.)* Brethren, resume your seats.

*(The W. M. should now stand for the presentation of the Warrant.)*

I. M.– W. M., I now deliver into your keeping the Warrant of the Lodge. It has been for many years entrusted to the hands of worthy and distinguished Brethren, and I am sure that in delivering it into your charge it will lose none of its lustre, but will be transmitted to your successor pure and unsullied as you now receive it. *(The W. M. may now sit.)*

I also present to you the Book of Constitutions, which I strongly commend to your serious perusal, for you will find there is scarcely a case of difficulty that can occur in the Lodge but what a reference to that book will not set you right.

These are the By-laws of the Lodge which I recommend you to have read at least once during your year of office, so that the Brethren may not plead ignorance of them.

*(In a Hall Stone Lodge the Jewel may here be transferred.)*

### The 250th. Anniversary Commemorative Jewel

I. M.– W. M., during the ceremony of installing you into the Chair of this Lodge, I had the honour of investing you with the Collar and Jewel of your office. In addition to the Square, that Collar is adorned with the Commemorative Jewel, indicating that the members of this Lodge played their part in establishing a Fund which commemorates the preservation of

Freemasonry, through two and a half centuries. The design of the Jewel embodies the central theme of the Arms first granted to the "Hole Crafte and Fellowship of Masons" in 1472.

As you are aware, the income from this very substantial Fund is placed at the disposal of the Royal College of Surgeons of England, to further research into the science of surgery, as a real and practical contribution for the betterment of the health and happiness of humanity.

I feel sure, W. M., the members will always feel great pride and satisfaction, that this adornment to the Master's Collar marks the Lodge's participation in this great enterprise.

I. M.– W. M., you will now please appoint and invest your Officers.

*The above is included by the kind permission of the Authors, The Provincial Grand Lodge of Surrey*

## *Appointment and Investiture of Officers.*

*(The D. of Cs. goes to the centre of the Lodge, and with the Stp. and Sn. of the First Degree says)–*

W. M., whom do you appoint your Senior Warden?

W. M., whom do you appoint your Junior Warden?

W. M., whom do you appoint Chaplain?

W. M., Wor. Brother *(name)* having been elected Treasurer, is it your pleasure to invest him?

W. M., whom do you appoint Secretary?

W. M., whom do you appoint Director of Ceremonies?

W. M., whom do you appoint Senior Deacon?

W. M., whom do you appoint Junior Deacon?

W. M., whom do you appoint Charity

Steward?

W. M., whom do you appoint Assnt. Director of Ceremonies?

W. M., whom do you appoint Almoner?

W. M., whom do you appoint Organist?

W. M., whom do you appoint Assnt. Secretary?

W. M., whom do you appoint Inner Guard?

W. M., whom do you appoint Stewards?

W. M., *(Wor.)* Brother *(name)*, having been elected Tyler, is it your pleasure to invest him?

*(The Bros. for the above offices should stand when named.)*

*(The D. of Cs. should then lead them to the correct side of the W. M. and after investment conduct them to their proper places.)*

*(The D. of C. should also conduct the P. Ms., acting S. W., J. W. and I. G. back to their places.)*

### *M. M.'s Investiture.*

TO SENIOR WARDEN

W. M.– Bro. ........, it affords me great pleasure to appoint you S. Warden of the

Lodge and to invest you with the Collar of your office, to which is attached a L., an emblem of equality, which points out the equal measures you are to pursue in conjunction with myself in the well ruling and governing of the Lodge. I hand you this column, which you will keep perpendicular while the Lodge is at labour, and horizontal when at refreshment. I also place in your hand this G . . l, an emblem of power, which will enable you to assist me in keeping order in the Lodge, particularly in the W. Your situation is in the W., and your duty to mark the setting Sun, to close the Lodge by my command, having seen that every Brother has had his due.

*It is also your duty, as well as your privilege, to attend the quarterly communications of Grand Lodge, that this Lodge may be properly represented.

TO JUNIOR WARDEN

Bro. ......., I have much pleasure in

**Should this Bro. have served the office of W. previously this may be omitted.*

appointing you J. Warden of the Lodge, and investing you with the Collar of your office, to which is attached a P., an emblem of uprightness, which points out the integrity of the measures you are to pursue in conjunction with myself and our Bro. S. Warden in the well ruling and governing of the Lodge; particularly that part of your duty which relates to the admission of visitors, lest by your neglect any unqualified person should gain admission to our assemblies, and the Brethren be thereby innocently led to violate their obligations. I place in your hand this column, which you will keep horizontal while the Lodge is at labour, and perpendicular when at refreshment. I also hand you this G . . l, an emblem of power, which will enable you to assist me in keeping order in the Lodge, particularly in the S., so that when I sound to order in the E., and our Bro. S. Warden in the W., you will respond in the S. Your situation is in the S., and your duty to mark the Sun at the meridian, to call the Brethren from labour to refreshment, and from refreshment to labour, that profit and pleasure may be the result. It is also your duty as well as your privilege, to attend the quarterly communications of Grand Lodge, that this Lodge may be properly represented.

*(Impromptu or as under.)*

TO CHAPLAIN

Bro. .........., I appoint you Chaplain of the Lodge and have the pleasure to invest you with the Jewel of your office.

The Jewel *(W. M. holds it)* is an open book on a twelve pointed radiated Star. It is symbolical of that great light in Freemasonry, the V. of the S. L. which should be a rule and guide to our faith.

The Star radiating in twelve directions points out the paths of happiness which may be found under the divine influence of the Sacred writings.

As Freemasons we are taught and recommended to contemplate with all seriousness the S. Volume and to consider it as the unerring standard of truth and justice. I trust therefore that whenever you invoke the blessing of the G. A. the Brn. will be reminded of our Ancient Charge.

*(Impromptu or as under.)*

TO TREASURER

Bro. ......., yours is an office of great trust and we are gratified by your election to the Office of Treasurer, and on behalf of the Lodge I invest you with the Collar and Jewel of your Office. It will be a pleasant satisfaction to you to feel that you have the esteem and confidence of your Brn., and I trust the duties you will be called upon to perform may have the reward of financial success for the good of the Lodge and the Charities we all admire.

*(Impromptu or as under.)*

TO SECRETARY

I appoint you Secretary of the Lodge and invest you with the Collar and Jewel, I thank you for accepting this office and the onerous duties attached to it.

It is an office which brings you personally in touch with every member of the Lodge, and it requires great tact, patience and geniality to be a successful Secretary.

The Secretary of the Lodge is often expected to be the encyclopaedia of

Masonic Constitution and I feel certain you will not be wanting in your anxiety to help any or all of us should we require it.

*(Impromptu or as under.)*

TO DIRECTOR OF CEREMONIES

Bro. .........., I appoint you Director of Ceremonies and invest you with the Collar and Jewel and hand you the Wand of your office. Your duty is to regulate our Ceremonies and to keep a careful eye on the working of the ritual.

It is also your duty to receive any distinguished Brn. and ensure their receiving the honours due to them.

TO SENIOR DEACON.

Bro ........, it gives me great pleasure to appoint you S. Deacon of the Lodge, and to invest you with the Collar and Jewel of your office, and placing in your hand this wand, the emblem of your office. Your situation is at, or near my right, and your duty to bear all messages and commands from myself to the S. Warden, and await the return of the J. Deacon. It is also your duty to attend the candidates during the ceremonies of Passing and Raising, and to assist the J. Deacon when required.

TO JUNIOR DEACON

Bro. ......., I have much pleasure in appointing you J. Deacon of the Lodge, and investing you with the Collar and Jewel of your office, also in placing in your hand this wand, the emblem of your office. Your situation is at the right of the S. Warden, and your duty to carry all my messages and communications from the S. to the J. Warden, and see the same punctually obeyed. It is also your duty to attend the candidates for Inititation, and to assist the S. Deacon when required.

TO CHARITY STEWARD

Bro. ......., I appoint you Charity Steward of the Lodge and I now invest you with the jewel of your office which is a trowel. The trowel is used in operative Masonry for cementing and bonding together the building or edifice. In speculative Masonry it can be likened to your duties of promoting and cementing among the Brethren of the Lodge their support to our

Masonic Charities, and may every blessing attend your labours.

(*Impromptu or as under.*)

TO ASST. D. OF C.

Bro. ......., I appoint you Assistant Director of Ceremonies of the Lodge, and invest you with the Collar and Collar Jewel, and hand you the Wand of your office. Your work will be to assist the D. of C. in the discharge of his duties, and at the same time familiarize yourself with the fuller duties of the D. of C. so that you are well able to perform them should you at any time be called upon.

(*Impromptu or as under.*)

TO ALMONER

Bro. ......., it gives me great pleasure to appoint you Almoner of the Lodge and invest you with your Collar, to which is attached a Jewel in the form of a scrip purse upon which is a heart, this being the emblem of your office. Your duties are to distribute the alms when necessary, and generally attend to the needs of those in sickness or distress whenever the occasion arises.

*(Impromptu or as under.)*

TO ORGANIST

Bro. ......, I appoint you Organist of the Lodge and invest you with the Collar and Jewel. Music is the most beautiful of the seven Arts and Sciences and has always borne an important part in all Rites and Ceremonies. It is a comfort in sadness and a stimulant to rejoicing.

It is therefore fitting that sweet sounds of harmony should be intermixed with the solemn influence of our ceremonies and thus typify the harmony and concord which should be the very essence of Freemasonry.

*(Impromptu or as under.)*

TO ASSISTANT SECRETARY

Bro. ........., I appoint you Assistant Secretary of the Lodge, and I now invest you with the Jewel of your office, which is two pens in saltire. Your duties are to assist the Secretary in the discharge of his work, and do everything that is possible to lighten his task.

TO INNER GUARD

Bro. ......, it gives me much pleasure to appoint you Inner Guard of the Lodge, and to invest you with the Collar and Jewel of your office. Your situation is within the entrance of the Lodge, and your duty to admit Freemasons on proof, receive candidates in due form, and obey the commands of the J. Warden. Although this is a subordinate office it is nevertheless a very important one, as on the tact and efficiency of the I. G. materially depends the smooth working of the Lodge business.

TO STEWARD

Bro. ......, I appoint you Steward of the Lodge and invest you with the Collar and Jewel of your office.

The Cornucopia, better known as the Horn of Plenty, is emblematical of the good things of this world which are necessary to our bodily strength; and it will be your duty to assist in providing the best available for the comfort of the Brethren.

May I remind you that you should endeavour to make yourself acquainted with the work of the Lodge so that in the absence of any officer, the D. of C. may rely on your assistance to fill a vacancy.

TO TYLER

*(W. M. G . . ls for Tyler, who enters, salutes and is conducted by the D. of C. to the correct side of the W. M., according to rank. He surrenders his Sword to the W. M., who lays it on the side of the Pedestal in a convenient position (never on the V. of the S. L.) whilst investing Tyler with Collar and Jewel.)*

Bro. ......, you having been elected Tyler of the Lodge, it affords me great pleasure to invest you with the Collar and to return you the Jewel of your office, which will enable you to keep off all Cowans and eavesdroppers to Freemasonry, and suffer none to pass save those duly qualified.

W. M. (*G . . ls here.*) (*Holding Sword and turning to the Brethren.*)

Brethren, the Sword symbolically teaches us to set a watch at the entrance of our thoughts, place a guard at the door of our lips, and post a sentinel in the avenue of our actions, thereby excluding every unworthy thought, word, or deed, thus preserving a conscience void of offence towards God and man.

END OF INVESTITURE OF OFFICERS

*(Three addresses are then given. For the first, the Installing Master stands at the left of the S. W.)*

I. M.– W. Bro. ......, you having been installed Master of this Worthy, Worshipful and Warranted Lodge, cannot be insensible to the obligations which devolve upon you as its head, nor of your responsibility for the faithful discharge of the duties annexed to the appointment. The honour, reputation, and usefulness of the Lodge, will materially depend on the skill and ability with which you manage its concerns, while the happiness of the Brethren will be promoted in proportion to the zeal and assiduity with which you promulgate the genuine principles and tenets of the Craft. As a pattern of excellence, consider that grand luminary the Sun, which, rising in the E., diffuses light and lustre to all within its circle. In like manner, W. M., it is your province to communicate light and instruction to the Brethren of the Lodge. Forcibly impress upon them the dignity and high importance of Freemasonry, seriously admonish them never to disgrace it, charge them to practice out of the Lodge those excellent precepts they are taught within it, and by virtuous, amiable, and discreet conduct, prove to the world the happy and beneficial effects of our ancient and honourable Institution, so that when a man is said to be a Freemason, the world may know that he is one to whom the burdened heart may pour forth its sorrow, to whom the distressed may prefer their suit, whose hand is guided by Justice, and whose heart is expanded by Benevolence. Finally, W. M., by a strict observance of the By-laws of the Lodge, the Constitutions of Freemasonry, and, above all, the V. of the S. L., that great light which is given as a rule and guide to our faith, you will be enabled to lay up a crown of joy and rejoicing which shall never fade, but remain until time with you shall be no more, and may the G. A. O. T. U. give you health, strength, and wisdom, to conduct the affairs of the Lodge with credit to yourself and to the satisfaction of its members.

*(Second Address from Secretary's table:)*

Bro. Wardens. *(Here Wardens stand.)* The W. Master having appointed you to the principal offices, you are to consider yourselves pledged by your acceptance thereof to a faithful discharge of your duties, and to a regular attendance during the time for which you have been appointed. You are so well acquainted with your duties to warrant any distrust that you will be found wanting in the discharge of them, suffice it to say that what you see praiseworthy in others you will carefully imitate, and what in them may appear defective, you will in yourselves amend. You ought to be examples of good order and regularity, as it is only by a due observance of the laws in your own conduct that you can reasonably expect obedience to them from others. You are assiduously to assist the W. Master in the discharge of the duties of his important trust, and carefully instruct those he may place under your care. In due course you may succeed to higher duties, your attainments therefore should be of such a nature that the Brethren may not suffer for want of proper instruction. From the zeal you have shewn towards our excellent Institution, and the desire you have evinced to promote its best interests, I entertain no doubt that your conduct will be such as to merit the approbation of the Brethren and the gratifying testimony of a good conscience.

*(Third Address, from the left of the W. M.:–)*

Brethren, such is the nature of our Constitution, that some must of necessity rule and teach, and others learn, submit, and obey, humility in each is an essential virtue. The Brethren whom the W. Master has selected to assist him in the well ruling and governing of the Lodge are too conversant with the laws of propriety, and the rules which govern our Ancient Institution to exceed the powers with which they have been entrusted, and you, my Brethren, are of too generous a disposition to envy their preferment. I therefore trust we shall have but one aim in view, to unite in the grand design of being happy and communicating happiness. May you enjoy every satisfaction and delight which disinterested friendship can afford and within these peaceful walls may your children, and your children's children, celebrate with joy and rejoicing the transactions of this auspicious solemnity. May Freemasonry flourish in every part of the world, and become influential in diffusing the light of Wisdom, aiding the strength of Reason, dispensing the blessings of Virtue, and lessening the aggregate of human misery and vice by extending the bounties of Charity to every deserving object under Heaven. Firm in rectitude, may it rise superior to all opposition, and, like the bleak mountain, which bares its crest with dignified composure to every tempest and fearlessly presents its bosom to the midnight storm; may it remain until time shall be no more, a perfect monument of Wisdom, Strength and Beauty, which ages cannot obliterate nor adversity decay.

Our Order, founded on the purest principles of Piety and Virtue, teaches us to regulate our actions by the rule of rectitude, square our conduct by the principles of morality, and guide our conversation – aye, even our very thoughts – within the compass of propriety; hence we learn to be meek, humble and resigned, to moderate those passions the excess of which deform and disorder the very soul; to be faithful to our God, our country, and our laws; it teaches our bosoms to beat high with the amiable sentiments of Honour, Truth and Virtue; to shed a tear of sympathy o'er the failings of a Brother, and pour the healing balm of consolation into the wounds of the afflicted. And the Brother, who has thus far discharged his duties as a Freemason, may patiently await the arrival of his dying throb, for we must all experience that awful change when the soul takes wing through that boundless and unexplored expanse, and may the G. A. O. T. U. say, "It is well finished," and admit us to the Grand Lodge above, where the divisions of time shall cease, and a glorious eternity burst open to our view.

Such, my Brethren. are the true principles of Freemasonry, such the beautiful tenets of the Craft, and may they be transmitted through our Lodges, pure and unsullied, from generation to generation.

THE END

*See special note on page 200*

## ***Presentation of Grand Lodge Certificate***

Now that you have been Raised to the Sublime Degree of a Master Mason you are entitled to receive a certificate, issued by the Most Worshipful Grand Master of the United Grand Lodge of England.

Brother (*name*) I now have much pleasure in presenting your Certificate to you in Open Lodge, (*hands it*) if you will kindly examine it, I will endeavour to explain some of its meaning.

Masonic history informs us that in all probability, certificates, of some form or another, were issued by individual Lodges from an early date. The standardised form of certificate was first introduced by the "Moderns" Grand Lodge in 1756. They later produced the "St. Paul's Certificate" in 1810, so named because of the prominence of Sir Christopher Wren's masterpiece in the design. The St. Paul's Certificate was adopted by the United Grand Lodge at its constitution in 1813, and issued until 1819, when the present "Pillars Certificate" was introduced.

Our Most Worshipful Grand Master, being a Prince of the Blood Royal, the Document is surmounted by the Royal Arms.

There next appears the Title or Style of our Order; "United Grand Lodge of Ancient, Free and Accepted Masons of England". This dates from the year 1813, when two rival Grand Lodges harmoniously joined together under the Grand Mastership of the Duke of Sussex, the 6th. Son of George the third.

The older of these two Grand Lodges, the "Moderns", was formed in 1717 by four London Lodges already established, and became the Mother Grand Lodge of the World.

In 1751, a number of Lodges, not approving the work of the Mother Grand Lodge, formed the "Antients" Grand Lodge. They claimed the appellation "Antients" because they chose to revert to old Practices disregarded by the earlier body, who they condemned as "Moderns". Happily the differences were finally dissolved in the formation of our present Constitution.

You will observe that the main feature of the design is the three great pillars. The centre one, of the Ionic Order, signifies Wisdom and alludes to the Wisdom of S., K. of I. in building, completing and dedicating the Temple at Jerusalem to the service of the G. A. of the U. . The Pillar on the left is of the Doric Order, which denotes Strength, and alludes to the strength of H. K. of T. in supporting K. S. with men and materials. That on the right is of the Corinthian Order, meaning Beauty: it refers to H. A., whose beautiful work in adorning the Temple was the admiration of all beholders.

These three pillars rest on the black and white flooring of the Lodge, symbolising the light and darkness, the joys and sorrows of our chequered existence.

On the floor are the three great emblematical lights in Freemasonry, the V. of the S. L., the S., and the Cs. . You will observe also, the W. Ts. of the three Degrees, the Tracing Board, the rough and perfect Ashlars, and the celestial and terrestrial Globes, pointing out Masonry Universal.

The wording states, to all whom it may concern, that the Brother referred to in the Certificate has been regularly received into our Order. The date is recorded Anno Lucis, or the year of Masonic Light; which preceded the Christian Era by four millenaries.

In testimony that the Brother's name has been registered in the Books of Grand Lodge, the Grand Secretary has subscribed his name and affixed the Seal of Grand Lodge. On this Seal, if you examine it closely, you will see certain Hebrew characters; they are "Kodesh Lo Adonai", meaning "Holiness to the Lord". There is also that excellent maxim of the Craft "Audi Vide Tace" which enjoins us to listen, observe, and remain silent.

A final clause states that possession of this Certificate does not entitle a Brother to admission into any Lodge without due examination. Neither, it should be noted, does examination alone give entrance without production of this voucher – should it be demanded. To the Brother to whom it is issued, this parchment, therefore is of unique value. It testifies that Grand Lodge considers the foundation stone, placed in the N. E. corner of the Lodge, not many months ago, was well and truly laid; it is a means of Masonic identification; a proof membership in case of accident or unforeseen calamity; a passport when visiting a foreign Lodge, where the signs differ from our own; and, even as no Lodge is "regular" without the production of the Warrant entrusted to its Master, so should no individual Mason omit to take his Certificate with him, when attending any special Masonic assembly; but I must warn you, it should not be framed or put on public exhibition.

Brother (*name*), your Certificate at present is incomplete. You are required to add your usual autograph in the space provided, and from that signature there must be no subsequent deviation. This you will do now in the N. of the Lodge at our Brother Secretary's table.

*(See special note on page 200.*
*Candidates should be informed again.)*

# *Comparison of Analogous Parts in the Three Degrees*

| | | |
|---|---|---|
| Now comes of his own free will and accord - - - | has made such progress as he hopes will recommend him to be Passed - - - - | has made such further progress as he hopes will recommend him to be Raised - - - - |
| Being free and of good report. | the assistance of the S. and the benefit of a P. G. and P. W. . | the united aid of the S. and Cs. and the benefit of a P. G. and P. W. |
| The T. of G. R. has already been heard i. h. f., do you Bro. I. G. vouch that he is properly prepared | We acknowledge the propriety of the aid b. w. h. s. a., do you Bro. I. G. vouch that he is in possession of the P. G. and P. W. | We acknowledge the powerful aid b. w. h. s. a., do you Bro. I. G. vouch that he is in possession of the P. G. and P. W. . |
| Thus assured you will K . . l. | Let the Candidate k . . l - - | Let the Candidate k . . l - - |
| Vouchsafe Thine aid A. F. S. G. of the Universe - - - | We supplicate the continuance of Thine aid O. M. L. - - | Almighty and Eternal God A. and R. of the Universe - - |
| Right glad am I to find - - | Let the Candidate rise. | Let the Candidate rise. |
| Brethren, in the N., E., S., and W., take notice - - - - | Brethren, take notice - - | Brethren, take notice - - |
| W. M. I present to you Mr. X., a Can. prop. pre'd to be made a Freemason. | W. M. I present to you Bro. Y., a Can. prop. pre'd to be passed to the 2nd Degree. | W. M. I present to you Bro. Z., a Can. prop. pre'd to be raised to the 3rd Degree. |
| Advance to the E. in due form. 3 stps | advance to the E. by the proper stps. 5 stps. | advance to the E. by the proper stps. 7 stps. |
| It is my duty to inform you - - - - | As in every degree the secrets of F. - - - - | It is but fair to inform you - - - - |
| K. on your Lt. K. - - - - | K. on your Rt. K. - - - - | K. on both. Ks. - - - - |

| | | |
|---|---|---|
| I (full name) in the presence of the G. A. O. T. U., and of this worthy, worshipful and warranted Lodge of A. F. and A. Ms., reg. assembled and properly dedicated - - - - | I (full name) in the presence of the T. G. G. O. T. U., and of this worthy and worshipful Lodge of F. C. Freemasons, regularly held assembled and properly dedicated - - - - | I (full name) in the presence of the T. M. H., and of this worthy and worshipful Lodge of M. Ms duly constituted, regularly assembled and properly dedicated - - - - |
| Solemnly and Sincerely swear - - - - | Solemnly promise and swear - - - - | Most solemnly promise and swear - - - - |
| any parts or parts, point or points, of the secrets and mysteries - - - - | any or either of the secrets and mysteries - - - - | any or either of the secrets and mysteries - - - - |
| I likewise solemnly promise that I will not write those secrets - - - | I further solemnly promise to act as a true and faithful Craftsman - - - | I likewise solemnly engage to adhere - - -<br>I further solemnly pledge myself to maintain and uphold - - - - |
| on the violation of any of them - - - - | on the violation of either of them - - - - | on the violation of either of them - - - - |
| So help me G., and keep me steadfast - - - - | So help me A. G., and keep me steadfast - - - - | So help me T. M. H., and keep me steadfast - - - - |
| As what have you repeated | As a pledge of fidelity | As a pledge of fidelity |
| Having been restored to the ….. of ….. ….. | Your progress in F. M. is marked by the position of | Let me once more direct your attention to the - - |
| I will add to the observation of our Bro. S. W. - - - | I will state that the badge with which you have now been invested - - - | I must state that the badge with which you have now been invested - - - - |
| You are now at liberty at retire - - - | You are now at liberty at retire - - - - | You are now entitled to take your seat in a M. Ms Lodge |

ISBN 978-0-85318-559-8

9 780853 185598